With gratitude to all who have mothered me

For Zion's sake I will not keep silent,
and for Jerusalem's sake I will not rest,
until her vindication goes forth as brightness,
and her salvation as a burning torch.

—ISAIAH 62:1

Contents

Foreword

The focus of this book is to help women understand their femininity and to live it more fully in everyday life. Is it not odd, then, that a man should be writing the foreword?

Obviously I don't speak with the authority of a woman. But I do speak as a man who has devoted his life to understanding, upholding and defending the dignity of women. This is the mission of every man. And how tragically men have failed—individually and collectively—in their mission, myself being first on the list.

Women very often find it difficult to embrace the gift of their femininity because of wounds men have caused in failing to honor them. A world that portrays women as objects for male pleasure is a world that puts women on the defensive, sometimes to the point where women subtly (or not so subtly) reject their own femininity as a means of self-protection.

If you have never heard this before from a man, it is a fitting way to set the stage for your reading of this book. Allow me, as a representative of the male side of the human race, to say how deeply sorry I am for the failures of men to love you, to honor you, to uphold and defend your dignity as a woman. Please forgive us. We know not what we do.

Oh, if both women and men could come to understand more fully the divine treasures revealed through the mystery of woman! *The Authentic Catholic Woman* certainly provides a good place to start.

Pope John Paul II, in his letter "On the Dignity and Vocation of Women," described woman as "the representative and the archetype of the whole human race." She is the one who "represents the humanity which belongs to all human beings, both men and women."[1]

Why? According to the great spousal analogy of the Scriptures, God wants to "marry" us—to live with us in an eternal union of love, which the Bible compares to a marriage. According to the analogy, God is the Bridegroom and humanity is the bride. God initiates the gift of love, and like a bride, all of humanity is called to open itself to receive God's love, conceive God's love and bear it forth to the world.

Not only does God want to "marry" us. Spousal love is something fruitful; it reveals the mystery of fatherhood and motherhood. In the spousal union of God with humanity, God wants to reveal the mystery of his own fatherhood in us. In a mystical way he wants to "impregnate" our humanity with his divine life.

This is obviously a very earthy way of speaking, and we need to be aware of the limitations of such an analogy. God, of course, is not sexual. Yet notice that this idea of being impregnated with divine life is not merely a metaphor. There was a woman who walked this planet who gave her yes so fruitfully to God's marriage proposal that she literally conceived divine life in her womb. In this way Mary reveals to us all what it means to be human, and all women share in that revelation and in that dignity.

To be human, once again, is an invitation to receive God's love, conceive God's love and carry it forth to others. This, in part, is the "theological message" of femininity. This, in part, is what makes woman the model of the whole human race.

Woman reveals the joy of being a creature, the joy of being receptive to the love of our heavenly Father and Bridegroom.

But what happens to woman's special "genius" if we conceive of God not as a loving Father and Bridegroom but as a jealous tyrant? Tragically, as a result of sin, woman's great blessing—her receptivity to life and love—has come to be seen as a curse.

Once again, nuptial imagery helps reveal why. Because of Satan's deception, we have come to see God's initiative as that of a tyrant, with a will to rule over us. Hence, in order not to be enslaved, we reject our posture of receptivity in favor of being our own "masculine" lords. We want to "'be like God,' but 'without God'" (*Catechism of the Catholic Church [CCC]*, 398). In this situation we come to see the "feminine"—which symbolizes our true humanity—as a weakness to be dominated and controlled, even snuffed out.

Does this not explain, perhaps, why there has been a tendency to favor masculinity over femininity throughout history? It seems that woman has been a constant reminder to the whole human race of what we in original sin rejected about ourselves— our receptivity before God. But the conception of God as tyrant-ruler—and in turn, the symbols of what is "masculine" (dominant slave-driver) and "feminine" (submissive slave)—are gross distortions.

In the fallen reality the man, rather than imaging the true initiative of God—rather than loving his wife "as Christ loved the church" (Ephesians 5:25)—comes to image the gross distortion of the tyrant-ruler: "[H]e shall rule over you" (Genesis 3:16). In turn, the woman, under the weight of male domination and history's discrimination against her, is tempted to reject her own femininity and take to herself the distorted "masculine" will to power, simply to survive.

Are these not some of the deepest reasons behind the women's liberation movement and the gender confusion so prevalent in our world today? The Church respects all that is good and just in the feminist movement. But in the words of John Paul II, the Church also calls women "to promote a 'new feminism' which rejects the temptation of imitating models of 'male domination,' in order to acknowledge and affirm the true genius of women in every aspect of the life of society, and overcome all discrimination, violence and exploitation."[2]

This is what makes Genevieve's book such a welcome contribution. Through a creative application of the principles found in John Paul II's theology of the body, Genevieve demonstrates that the life and gifts of the Church provide a map for living femininity to the full. She makes the theology of woman practical and demonstrates that women need not be afraid to be *women*. Women need not be afraid to give their "yes" to God with the same abandon Mary did. Only through this feminine "yes" can we build a culture of life and a civilization of love.

Lord, I pray that you would bless everyone who reads this book. I pray that you would open women's eyes in new ways to their own particular dignity and genius and inspire men to uphold every woman's dignity even to the shedding of his blood. Let it be, Lord, according to your will.

Christopher West
Fellow, Theology of the Body Institute

Overview:
What Do Women Want?

Countless people have asked this intriguing question, for countless reasons. Men ask it, wondering how to meet the needs of the women in their lives, often despairing of ever really understanding what makes women tick. Marketers ask it in order to find what will sell consistently and profitably to female consumers. Employers ask it in the context of how to satisfy female employees and bring out the best in their work potential. Educators ponder this question in order to meet the needs of female students and develop their gifts and talents.

Women even wonder about themselves and their friends, especially after reaching certain goals that they thought would give them a measure of happiness, only to find that an empty feeling remains deep in their souls.

We must start with the premise that each woman means well, that she begins with the best of intentions and that when treated with dignity and respect she will respond with her best effort. The dilemma is where to expend that effort. Often, women themselves don't know where to use their energies or don't realize what is going wrong with particular efforts that leave them feeling unhappy or frustrated. The mass media serves to confuse them even more with materialistic answers or empowerment messages that are ultimately unhelpful and false.

If God made us, then certainly He will know what will satisfy women and what will feed them spiritually. Thus we must return to God to see what His plan for women entails. In the following pages we will find the paradigm that includes all women, guides all women and focuses all women on the will of God for their lives. We will then consider what it takes to trust in this paradigm and where the basic obstacles lie. Finally, we must weigh the demands of authentic femininity against the price of rejecting it.

We live in a fallen world, and there are failings in every sector of society: on the part of men, in individual members of the Church and in the societal structures themselves. Everyone's choices have impact beyond the individual or representative group. There are books that address these other parties, and these have a critical place in the ongoing discussion on womanhood.

This book has a specific and limited scope. We will look at the ways that women can improve themselves and enhance the presence of authentic femininity in the world. This work is intended to be simply our piece of the puzzle that, when complete, will reveal a better understanding of the divine plan as it concerns the vocation of woman.

God wants our happiness; He wants our success. He wants us to find meaning in our lives, to fall into bed at night satisfied that our mental, physical and spiritual energies were spent in the right way.

I have offered this message to women in quiet ways over the years, and many women have received it with gratitude and joy. It is a message based on truth that I want to share with you, dear reader. What follows in these pages is the essence of femininity: where we will find our true home and God's richest blessings.

CHAPTER ONE

The Essence of Femininity

Among all of the challenges of our fallen world, in this generation the misunderstandings about the God-given gift of human sexuality are paramount, and correcting them is the preeminent battle of our day. Supermarket checkout stands, the offerings at the local mall and a sampling of the airwaves at any time of the day confirm the sad truth that sexual utilitarianism is flagrant, acceptable and well-packaged.

The human person—made in the image and likeness of God and capable of deep intimacy, heroic virtue and creative thought—is constantly reduced to his lowest appetites in the popular culture. He is stripped of most of his potential and asked to respond readily to his animal urges, tempted to see and use the people around him as conveniences and objects. While there is no possibility that this way of living can satisfy the human heart, its attractiveness has been systematically promoted to several generations with little significant opprobrium. The fallout has been massive. The loss of souls and the destruction of the family are the ultimate, unfortunate effects.

Few, if any of us, have escaped unharmed. Since the fall from grace of our first parents in the Garden, tension has been at the heart of human relationships, especially male-female relationships. With this tragic blueprint established and the original unity between man and woman breached, the ensuing lack of communion causes each to suffer the consequences in a unique way.

Adding more fuel to the fire in recent years are two rather unique things: the availability of certain medical technologies in the field of reproductive health and the predominance of a mass media that is efficient at spreading a variety of messages that weaken the family culture. Both of these elements have served to undermine the union between the conjugal act and its intended corollaries: lifelong bonding and procreation. With the dissolution of the natural link between the marital embrace and children, we see the inevitable destruction of the family unit and the disastrous consequences for women and children, who are more vulnerable without the stability of the family that God intended for their protection.

If we take a moment to consider the two-thousand-year history of the Church, which Jesus gave to us as custodian of eternal truths, it is evident that there have been constant misunderstandings, dilemmas and heresies to which her magisterium has had to respond with clarity and wisdom. In mission work and in exercising zeal for souls, the Church has always been *proactive*, stepping out with bold initiatives and inspired gestures of faith. But when it comes to the content of that faith, the Church is *reactive*, responding with prayer, great deliberation and a cohesive methodology of building on revealed truths and established dogma.

There have been many attacks—on Christ, the Trinity, the Blessed Mother, the hierarchy and the nature of the sacraments, to name some of the major areas of disagreement over the centuries. Each has brought about in its wake an ever-deepening awareness of God's plan and its implications for His creatures.

It is no different in our present age, when the contemporary attack happens to be in response to the fact that, from the dawn of creation, "male and female he created them" (Genesis 1:27).

The Church's response, which we have the privilege of witnessing, is a flowering of our understanding of human sexuality, the theology of the body, and the richness that it provides as a reflection of both the nature of God and the nature of man.

Pope John Paul II pioneered much of this deeply satisfying study. We owe an enormous debt of gratitude to him for his generous response to the grace of God in providing for his flock critical and penetrating insights into this subject. But he is not alone in this new springtime of understanding. We are witnessing a growing treasury of wisdom concerning the nuptial foundations of all of creation, the nuptial meaning of the human body and the great joy that is inherent in our dignity as participants in God's communion of love and redemption.

WOMAN'S ROLE IN THIS STRUGGLE

The implications for women are of great importance because, whether we like it or not, the choices we make are pivotal in the battle over the human heart. Throughout history, societies have tried myriad ways to construct familial and tribal patterns so as to build a larger, functioning society—but with varying degrees of justice toward the human person. Where these solutions do not apply the light of revealed truth and the effects of grace, it has proven impossible to build a stable and lasting civilization.

It is through families everywhere that culture is received, enriched and passed on from one generation to the next, primarily through the work of women. The woman is the very heart of civilization, and hence she—every woman—is the direct target of the enemies of a healthy family culture. The sexual revolution and the culture of death could not exist without the cooperation of women (through their willing adoption of ideologies contrary to the truth or through their unwilling corruption).

In reverse, the restoration of women to their proper dignity will have the critical effect of restoring the culture of life that our world so desperately needs. This was made clear at the Second Vatican Council in the closing message addressed to women:

> As you know, the Church is proud to have glorified and liberated woman, and in the course of the centuries, in diversity of characters, to have brought into relief her basic equality with man. But the hour is coming, in fact has come, when the vocation of woman is being achieved in its fullness, the hour in which woman acquires in the world an influence, an effect, and a power never hitherto achieved. That is why, at this moment when the human race is undergoing so deep a transformation, women impregnated with the spirit of the gospel can do much to aid mankind in not falling.[1]

This restoration of authentic feminine dignity must have as its foundation a way of living for women that is based on certain truths about their vocation. If this foundation is based on externals, on a shallow understanding of woman's worth, on false definitions of love or on humanly constructed stereotypes, women will not be able to stand against the lies and temptations that challenge them on a constant basis.

TEMPTATIONS

Indeed, there are three temptations that face all of us as we look at what it means to be women.

One is the tendency that we have to look backward, idealizing a particular bygone generation that seems to have avoided the excesses of the present age. Some who lament the corruption of the family look fondly at the era right after the Second World War, before children were prey to all sorts of modern influences, when divorces were few and parish life seemed strong. Some prefer to muse about the Victorian period, when mothers were queens in their homes and there was a rigorous moral code to which (at least externally) popular culture paid homage. There are even those with a broader grasp of history who idealize the medieval era or even the early centuries of the Church for their simplicity of life, certain freedoms of ministry for women and the Catholic culture established throughout Christendom.

Each age, it is true, has many strengths, and it is more than nostalgia that hearkens to a time that accepted without question the basic truths we are so weary of fighting for. Yet time is a continuum, and the temptation to slip backward is not good. We are personally called by our loving God to live in *this* particular generation—for better or worse. He offers us the graces to wage the war with sin in this place and under these circumstances. We have the potential to build the kingdom in our very midst. We must look squarely at the present and the future in order to live a vigorous and timely faith.

On the other hand, there is the temptation to abandon the past—the riches of the Church, the treasures of our culture and the wisdom of the ages—denying that anything that has gone before us can have any possible meaning for this generation. One might ask, for example, how could the teachings of the Church Fathers have any bearing on reproductive technologies when the early Christians had no grasp of our scientific techniques and extraordinary advances in medicine? Some, in fact, would see the challenges of our era as so unique that past models—especially of womanhood—are irrelevant and completely unhelpful in directing meaningful lives.

This tendency is as dangerous as the former. It overlooks the truths that endure throughout all generations and the timeless nature of man with his innate inclinations and needs. It robs the human person of the richness of experience, which confirms to the faithful that God is stronger than any lie, no matter how prevalent or well disguised.

The Holy Spirit always leads the Church, and what He has revealed to those who preceded us provides an essential and firm foundation for us and for those who will follow. Technology and innovation are often helpful, but they will not change either God or man. Often they suspend the need for people to face the most basic questions concerning life and death, of which the Church reminds us both in season and out.

Beyond these two extremes, the final danger for women is to create for themselves unrealistic images of piety that no mortal can imitate. Often, with an overdose of false humility and an entrenched stereotype of "the perfect Catholic woman," a well-meaning woman will imagine that the ordinary shortcomings in her personal life prohibit her from achieving personal sanctity. Many wrongly assume that authentic femininity means a blissful marriage, abundant pious (and well-mannered) children, a husband to rival Saint Joseph, an orderly home, a variety of community and parish activities, an even temperament, ample time for spiritual and corporal works of mercy, cheerful generosity toward an extended family (also pious, of course) and a prayer life patterned on that of any number of saints or mystics. This sort of conjecture can indeed be a woman's worst enemy.

Reason, human nature and original sin beg us to reconsider. Popular culture has significantly affected our understanding of holiness—and reality. Beautiful magazines, model homes and airbrushed media role models combine dangerously with our Calvinistic tendencies to link struggles and defects with God's disfavor. The foundations of much of our history, especially in the United States, are colored by a misreading of grace and redemption, which offered clean living and the Protestant work ethic as the path to comfort and success.

Where does this leave the woman with an alcoholic husband, fallen-away children or a chronic illness that limits all of her visible contribution to society? Only the fullness of faith—with its understanding of the economy of grace—and a realistic paradigm can give us a path based on truth and authentic femininity.

THE ESSENCE OF LIVING THE FAITH

Before considering this paradigm, it would be best to establish the essence of living a holy Christian life—for men and women. In brief, our Christian commitments fall in three categories.

A faithful Catholic is *loyal to the magisterium*. This requires an ongoing formation that takes us beyond childhood catechesis and establishes an adult understanding of our faith. Assent to the basic outlines of the faith—such as the nature of the Trinity, the need for redemption, the sacraments and the hierarchy—leads to discernment of the perpetual struggle between our wayward will and the will of God, as revealed through Holy Scripture, an active prayer and sacramental life and loving service of neighbor.

There is a certain docility that allows us to accept what we have yet to understand. This trust is founded on the virtues of hope (recognizing what we have seen and learned as evidence of a loving God true to His promises) and faith (knowing God will meet us on this journey toward understanding and provide the graces we need to persevere).

Secondly, since our God is a God of love and the natural outcome of love is fecundity, a faithful Catholic must be *open to life* according to his or her state in life. This openness is based on the dignity of the human person (being created in freedom and endowed with a rational nature), on his or her circumstances and on the recognition that life is a continuum from conception until natural death. Hence there are abundant possibilities as to how this fruitfulness will play out in individual lives.

Finally, an authentic Catholic should have a *personal relationship with the Blessed Mother*. Mary is the first pilgrim who trod this path of faith, the first fruit of our redemption and the most perfect image of the Church. She is more than just the woman on the greeting cards at Christmastime: She is the mother of our Savior, the very mother Christ gave to us as one of His most beautiful gifts just before He died (see John 19:26–27). She is a real companion to each Catholic in his or her life of complexities and challenges. Though a Catholic can achieve heaven without ever saying a rosary, focusing exclusively on Christ, we can find a greater depth of understanding and relationship to God through study of and affection for Our Lady, "our tainted nature's solitary boast."[2]

AUTHENTIC WOMEN

With all of these foundations established for living out a rich faith, it remains for us to find the model for women, which will help us not only to be truly Catholic but also to be truly feminine and distinct from men. This requires a template with two important attributes: It must be universal (that is, pertaining to all women) and tangible enough to have firm meaning for every woman. It must highlight both the fundamental equality of the sexes and their complementarity without being limited culturally. It cannot exclude any corner of the globe; thus it must be able to separate essential characteristics from accidentals. Neither is it limited spiritually. Two thousand years of Church history have revealed an abundance of valid charisms, and we must be open to the possibility of other legitimate expressions of faith in the future. In short, what we seek is a universal template that is truly catholic and available to women of all times and places.

As hard as it is to imagine, that paradigm does exist: It is the Church herself—the bride of Christ, born from His side on the cross—whose ministers the Holy Spirit commissioned on Pentecost to bring the gospel to all peoples. In the very first weeks of his pontificate, Pope John Paul II noted:

The Church of Jesus Christ and of the Apostles is at the same time a Church that is Mother and Spouse. These biblical expressions clearly reveal how deeply the mission of women is inscribed in the mystery of the Church. And may we discover together the many-sided significance of this mission—going hand in hand with the world of women today, and basing ourselves on the riches which from the beginning the Creator placed in the heart of Women.[3]

What the proper model does for women is to free them to use their God-given gifts. Each person is born into a unique set of circumstances—time, place, family, resources—and with a unique set of qualities, such as talents, inclinations, education and disposition. With the Church as model, the woman is free from crippling comparisons and can face God as an individual called to touch particular lives, and can discern His specific call to her.

All the wisdom of the ages is available for her to draw upon. Yet she knows that her response in love is unrepeatable and not subject to censure by those who have their own paths or vocations to pursue. In living out her particular image of the Church and staying prayerfully focused solely on its criteria, she is not bound or distracted by her mother, her neighbor or even her best friend. She is free to embrace her own path with its own challenges, tribulations and joys. In this paradigm, practically speaking, every woman can find the meaning of her unique vocation and her very essence as a daughter of God.

POWER TO TRANSFORM

If we take the time, in these pages and beyond—through prayer, meditation and creative initiatives—to look at all the dimensions of the Church, it will become more and more clear what it means to "image" the Church and how to make it the standard for our decision and our actions—indeed, how we live out every moment of our lives as women. Our study will encompass the specifics of the Church: her four marks; the seven sacraments; the Church as mother and teacher; the Church as virgin and bride, font of wisdom and inspirational source of culture; the physical church building itself, which is a life-giving sanctuary. Then we will look at the challenges to femininity: how our nature often hinders us; what traps we fall into when we reach out to those we love; how original sin corrupts our relationships, especially with men, undermining our attempts to love.

Through all of this I hope to present more fully the nuptial meaning of the body—indeed, the spousal realities that echo throughout all of creation and redemption—that these may become more and more alive for you. This meaning will unleash your receptivity as a woman, which is essential to how you receive and pass on love.

You are a feminine apostle—a vocation that has a startling richness and is distinct from both masculine apostles and false, weaker visions of womanhood. Through the true understanding of how woman makes a gift of herself to the created world, you can transform your faith and the lives of all those in your path.

You will also find available the graces you need to face the inevitable consequences of this transformation. Pain is unavoidable in this path of authentic feminine discipleship. In a particular way we must look at the vulnerabilities that women face and how to heal and forgive. Many times a woman internalizes her pain, unsure of what she as a good Christian should do about it. The ability to name the hurt, to forgive the offender and to move on is critical to a woman's ability to live out her vocation fully and to bring others to healing and wholeness as well. This takes great courage—and great trust. We have to beg for the graces to do this so that we can be all that God wants us to be.

This is a critical time for women and a critical time for the world. The Church has made it clear that if we women can discover the richness of our vocation, then we will have an impact that we never imagined. If we are faithful to our femininity, we can do what God asks of us and rebuild a civilization of love and life.

CHAPTER TWO

Mirroring the Sacraments of Initiation

A woman's work is never done" is a truism to which we can all relate. Whether she pulls a paycheck or not, there is a sense in which a woman feels responsible for both her physical surroundings and the needs of the persons near her. She cannot help but notice various features of her environment, and often she struggles with whether to respond and how—sensing issues of domain, justice and exhaustion. Many times a woman will not respond for one reason or another and then wonder if she acted appropriately.

Catholics have known from the start that all that we do matters; whether or not anyone acts (or refrains from acting) and with what disposition of heart has a bearing on building the kingdom. The fact that God chose to "pitch His tent" in this world means for us that every work—even the most mundane— has a spiritual significance for ourselves and others.

The theology behind this is "incarnational." The incarnation of the Word of God—Jesus' taking on human flesh—allows us to lift human actions and enfold them in grace, joining them to His own sacrifice of love. We should recognize the privilege it is to join in Christ's redemptive work. While we must be certain not to confuse this with "earning heaven" (which is impossible), this reality is both an incomprehensible mystery and a gracious gift of our loving God.[1]

One by one we'll consider the sacraments and how they are used to build up the mystical body of Christ, and then it will become obvious how the everyday lives of women naturally mirror them. In this chapter in particular we will look at the three sacraments of hospitality, or initiation.

When we appreciate how our work fits into God's plan of salvation, we can also establish some criteria that will help to gauge the best response to the needs around us. We can thus clarify the whole "hand-wringing" incidence of guilt, which can be very confusing and even debilitating. God does not want that for His daughters. Rather He wants us to meditate on the sacraments as channels of grace and reflect the supernatural life of the Church with our gifts of self, offered in love.

BAPTISM

The sacrament of baptism has two implications for the soul involved. The *Catechism* teaches, "Through Baptism we are freed from sin and reborn as sons of God; we become members of Christ, are incorporated into the Church and made sharers in her mission" (CCC, 1213). Thus we perceive the twofold effect of washing the person free of the stain of original sin and welcoming him or her into the Christian community. In everyday terms, since we wish to find ways to mirror the Church in an incarnational way, this dimension of the Church would be found ultimately in our efforts at cleaning and hospitality—which we easily recognize as two mainstays in the lives of women.

CLEANING IN THE SPIRIT OF CHRIST

It is almost comical to ask if cleaning is a part of our everyday activity. One dimension of the fall from grace is the chaos and disorder we inherited. Entropy reigns, and even good works are undone by time and the elements. From kitchen counters to beds, from noses to bottoms—nothing stays clean or in proper order for long.

Beyond the basic requirements of food, clothing and shelter, every culture has sought to keep disorder at bay. It is most often women who spend time, energy and resources on advancing the cause of cleanliness, order and even beauty. A constant source of irritation to all but the most saintly among us is that the good efforts we put into ordering our lives—making our surroundings attractive and cleaning for the sake of health—so quickly deteriorate into filth and disarray. Even when the human person is not directly to blame, the elements themselves break down: Dust and dirt appear, decay sets in and food becomes stale. What comes to mind is Sisyphus, forever pushing the enormous rock up the mountain only to have it come crashing down to the bottom just before reaching the top.

While Christians are mindful of the fact that this world is not our true home and that sin prevents the establishment of utopia, it is here that we can mirror the sacrament of baptism in the realm outside the soul. It is God's gift to us that we can lift up our mundane tasks of washing and purifying and link them to Christ's own work. What infinite meaning we can add to mopping up that spilled drink or cleaning out the broom closet one more time if we remember that we are imaging the sacrament of baptism.

To gain a better perspective, imagine the arenas in which women have worked at this over the millennia. In sunbaked deserts, frozen tundras, sweltering jungles and windswept prairies, what exhausting lengths women have had to go to in order to find water and maintain their humble surroundings. Some images from literature and history come to mind: battling the dust of the Australian outback, hanging laundry on lines strung between tenement buildings, creating order among the creeping wagon trains heading west on the American frontier, keeping sanitary the poor shacks of Southern slavery. If we compare our modern lives with its many conveniences to so many who have gone before us, we will see that it is at least easier now to tackle germs and debris.

Still we face the dreary fact that cleanliness must be pursued according to contemporary standards, whether it suits us or not, whether we'll be appreciated or not and whether it will lead to lasting order or not. Disorder, just like sin, weighs us down hourly, daily, perpetually, and we must attack it with our trash barrels, vacuums and washrags till the trumpet sounds, signaling the consummation of the world.

In all honesty, what are our choices? We can clean it, or we can leave it unclean. With the latter being contrary to our hopes for a civilized life, the next choice is either to clean and join our effort to the work of Christ, or to clean and wallow in bitterness and self-pity. (Then there is the completely valid option of paying to have someone else clean for us. Odds are that this "someone else" will be a woman if the work has to do with the home or with children. And then the option is hers to have this mission of cleaning in the image of the Church.)

Stories about the late Mother Teresa abound, and one in this vein concerns a particular town in Russia. The authorities finally had invited the Missionaries of Charity into the country and even allowed them to work in a local hospital, but at the outset they were not allowed into the areas of the building where the patients were. Instead they were relegated to cleaning toilets—a task that they embraced without argument.

Day in and day out they scrubbed in the nastiest of conditions, and they offered up this work with their prayers for the apostolate. Unaware of their presence, the hospital staff underwent a subtle transformation: They began to speak civilly to one another, acts of kindness multiplied and the atmosphere changed to reflect the warmth of genuine charity. In a matter of time the nuns were invited to minister to patients. The humility of the sisters and their ability to lift up even "latrine duty" forged a path that would bear more visible fruit later.

How many congregations of consecrated women have faced that inevitable first day in new quarters—complete with mops, buckets, brooms and scrub brushes? Consider the warm and welcoming nuns over the centuries who have greeted their often malnourished and affection-starved students with a quick trip to the nearby hand pump or sink to wash up. How many mothers have tackled bedroom after bedroom, wondering at the abysmal living standards of their own dear children? How much of every mother's day is spent keeping up with the trails of crumbs, the jam-smeared faces and the mounds of soiled laundry—no doubt grateful for not having to beat it on rocks in the local stream?

A beautiful point of reflection for this image are the women in Christ's life who ministered to Him, primarily the Blessed Mother. She washed and swaddled Him countless times from the start and no doubt did it each time with great care and reverence. Imagine the attention with which she wiped the food from His face and the soil from his hands as a child.

Later Veronica would wipe the sweat and blood from His face during the Passion, and others would attend to His lifeless body after the Crucifixion. Several women were privileged to wash and anoint His corpse, and we know that, amid the tears and heartache, the whole event was laden with both natural and supernatural beauty.

What we must avoid is the pride involved in setting ourselves up as "too good" to simply clean. Even Christ washed His disciples, establishing an extraordinary precedent: God cleaning dirty human feet. Being too busy, being involved with other work or utilizing other gifts can certainly excuse one from much of the tedious and humble work of cleaning. Nevertheless we always will have opportunities to clean and provide order. It is for us to link this action with the sacraments. Both baptism and reconciliation are pertinent here, as the ongoing cleansing involved in regular confession is another backdrop for the endless work we have before us.

HOSPITALITY

The other dimension of baptism that has a direct bearing on the vocation of women is the welcome that the faith community provides for newly baptized souls. The implication for the feminine vocation is our call to establish a "habit of hospitality." As the Church reminds us that human life is a continuum from conception until natural death, so our welcome to the human person must span that complete spectrum according to the events that unfold in our family and in society at large.

From welcoming a new infant to creating a place in our lives for the needs of the elderly, women can provide an essential forum of love and comfort for all. This invitation is going to vary with each woman, according to her state in life; the circumstances she lives with, her talents and her means will all affect her call in this area. In prayer she can come to discern which souls God is calling her to embrace.

For a student this may mean a kind word or understanding smile for a difficult classmate; for a working woman it can mean a generous spirit in the office or factory; for a wife it may be a call to receive new life. These actions begin with basic charity but must be taken a step further to bear authentic good intentions for each soul and concern for his or her well-being.

In many neighborhoods now there are few doors open on any given day, few places where a child roaming on a bicycle can find a friendly face. In our fast-paced world, how many times do we seek warm human connections only to find brusque responses or impersonal encounters? Even establishing eye contact with a sales clerk is often difficult. Monotony is the price of efficiency.

What a difference women can make by being open to the human person, being sensitive to his or her needs and generous enough to offer a gift of self—even if it's just a quick motherly smile or an understanding comment. Sometimes these small actions make all the difference in someone's day. Meanwhile we recognize that the needs of some are going to demand much more of us. Prayer and prudence are necessary as we consider our resources.

While there are examples everywhere of such hospitality, the nearly contemporary story of Saint Gianna Beretta Molla is both inspirational and pertinent, particularly in this age when children often are seen as burdens unworthy of our heroic sacrifices. In September 1961, at the age of thirty-nine, this doctor was pregnant with her fourth child when she was diagnosed with a uterine tumor.

In Gianna's mind there were no options other than to give every opportunity for life and good health to her "guest." When her doctor suggested an abortion, she rejected it out of hand, saying, "I shall accept whatever they will do to me provided they save the child." Knowing fully the weight of this decision, she prayerfully and joyfully offered her life, if necessary, for the safety of her daughter.

Gianna underwent surgery in a way that would not be harmful to the child. She went on to deliver her daughter full term on Holy Saturday, April 21, 1962. Gianna died seven days later, having given a magnificent witness to her family, her community and the world at large.

The daughter, Gianna Emmanuela, has tried to express the great lesson of her mother: "Dear Mom, thank you for having given me life two times: when you conceived me and when you permitted me to be born, protecting my life…. And so my life seeks to be the natural continuation of your life."[2]

This daughter, as well as Gianna's husband and two of her other children, were present in Rome at the beatification on April 24, 1994. There Pope John Paul alerted the world to take heed of this selfless act of hospitality: "By holding up this woman as an exemplar of Christian perfection, we would like to extol all those high-spirited mothers of families who give themselves completely to their family, who suffer in giving birth, who are prepared for every labor and every kind of sacrifice, so that the best they have can be given to others."[3]

Such is the nature of hospitality that we should give in love, understanding that it is not a fruitless oblation. Harboring souls and nourishing them are tangible reflections of Holy Mother Church and must reflect the same constancy of spirit. Only God's grace can support such generosity, as His life fuels life in the body of Christ.

While men are called to hospitality in their own way, this is a special call to women. When we discover a harsh or difficult man, we may be put off or disappointed, but not to the degree that we are shaken when we encounter a woman who is closed to the human person. A cold, impersonal woman can rattle us to the core, because we instinctively hope for warmth and welcome.

Hollywood and television have consistently played on the foil of the heartless woman for the sake of her shock value. Such characters perplex and fascinate audiences in many arenas, but no one wants to have to deal with such a woman on a regular basis. Rather we hope that women, as images of the Church, will provide at least some semblance of comfort—much like the relief we find on visiting the nearby church and finding the door unlocked and the tabernacle lamp lit. The Church has long been considered a sanctuary, and it is this very welcome that women need to image as they place themselves at the service of the human person.

A woman who seeks to provide hospitality on as wide a scale as possible must prioritize her actions so that openness to one never encumbers openness to another who has more of a claim on her time and energy. In this respect we should consider the testimony of one family's children who were regularly turned out of their beds when guests appeared, left hungry for the sake of strangers at the table and deprived of their parents' affections for the sake of misplaced hospitality. Resentment grew in this family because the parents overlooked the fact that their children were their initial "guests," and charity demanded that they comfort and console them in due proportion.

This is not to say that parents and children cannot conspire to sacrifice comforts for the sake of others in corporate fashion. But we cannot overlook the formation of our own offspring in generosity, or we will have neglected our primary duties.

Money, while enhancing one's ability to be hospitable, is not the key factor. More important is the disposition of the heart. Keep in mind that most people who come knocking at the door are seeking a personal encounter, not fine food or a sophisticated atmosphere. Some hostesses tend to cripple themselves by binding these elements together in varied ways—consider Martha. The food does have its place (as we'll see when looking at how the Eucharist fits into the feminine vocation), but hospitality is founded first and foremost on love, an irreplaceable gateway to souls, which will clear the path for God to work.

THE EUCHARIST

The sacrament of the Eucharist builds upon the hospitality of baptism in that it nourishes with a supernatural banquet the souls that have been welcomed into the mystical body of Christ. The *Catechism* teaches us that "[t]hose who receive the Eucharist are united more closely to Christ. Through it Christ unites them to all the faithful in one body—the Church. Communion renews, strengthens, and deepens this incorporation into the Church, already achieved by Baptism" (CCC, 1396).

Here we see that the reception of Holy Communion fortifies the critical element of unity. The marvelous interchange of gifts in baptism and the Eucharist deepen our relationship with Christ and with one another.

As we look at the Eucharist in all of its dimensions, we will find our plan of action and understand how our femininity will be linked to the building of the kingdom. Certainly the Eucharist is a meal, and meals are something with which we are intimately familiar. But a meal is more than the provision of mere physical sustenance; it is the opportunity for us to share in a personal and spiritual communion with those given to us by God.

As Christ gives Himself to us, we give of our very selves as we feed others. This can begin in the womb for those who are given the gift of motherhood, at the breast for those who so choose to feed their infants, at the dinner table, the picnic table, the soup kitchen, spoonful by spoonful in a nursing home and in every other setting where those who hunger are nourished.

In imitation of the magnanimous generosity of her Spouse, the Church prepares the banquet, and so must we as women whenever we are so called. By giving food and drink in His name (as we are reminded by the teaching on the corporal works of mercy in Matthew 25:31–46), we are not only giving to persons in need but returning to Christ what is by rights already His.

Thus gratitude to God must be part of the premise before we begin "saying grace" at the table. With grateful hearts we should recognize how blessed we are to have anything at all to prepare and offer our loved ones. While we are often overwhelmed with the parade of meals to prepare and even with the display of choices in the supermarket, consider how blessed we are in this generation to have such a wide array of fruits, vegetables, meats and ready-to-eat entrées year-round. Many of our ancestors (and even contemporary neighbors) have suffered from hunger or—in the best of times—monotony.

So, in our typically feminine way, women receive from God the ability to feed themselves and others, and they see Him in the faces of those they nourish. This is not to ignore the reality of the drudgery, the common ingratitude of those receiving the gifts and the physical and emotional strains such provisions require. What we have to focus on is the sacramental richness hidden behind the veil of ordinary life, which gives meaning and value to these acts of love.

Would that we were always grateful and aware of the gift we receive in the Eucharist—truly God Himself—but in honesty we know that we are not. Perhaps if we are mindful that we fall short in our own appreciation of God's abundant generosity, we will have patience with those who fail to acknowledge the little we do for them.

While understanding that the imitation of this sacrament embraces all forms of nourishment—physical as well as spiritual—it will be sufficient here to dwell on the family meal, since so many women participate in providing this for their loved ones. In talking of authentic love, it is important to remember that there are two dimensions: the ability to give generously and the ability to receive. Both are essential, and both must be integrated into the gift of nourishing others. The exchange must be recognized as mutual and even inherently perpetuating, since after passing along what a woman receives from God, she also may be nourished by her guests in the measure to which she remains open.

It is certainly possible to give in a sort of isolated, egocentric manner, forcing the gift according to our own needs, tastes and timetable, but this is not the way Christ would have us give. He wants us to live for others and to give generously according to the needs of others, understanding of course that formation and schooling in sanctity are often a portion of what others—especially children—ultimately need.

For a truly mutual exchange, therefore, before giving to others we must receive them in love so that there is authentic communion. They may have a contribution to the gathering we did not anticipate (or need), and graciously receiving them and what they bring to the table is essential.

This idea reflects the Offertory of the Mass, where the faithful are called to bring their gifts to the altar so that they may be fed in turn by Christ Himself. This Offertory rite, in fact, created an enormous obstacle to one convert to the Church. Rosalind Moss had made the great leap from Judaism to Protestantism, but in her inquiry into Catholicism she was stymied by the concept of an "exchange of gifts." She was scandalized that God would have *need* of our gifts to complete the perfect sacrifice of Christ offered in atonement for our sins.

Finally Rosalind found a priest who explained this exchange by illustration. He asked her to imagine a mother preparing a cake and being approached by a small child who wanted to help. The mother certainly wouldn't need the help of her daughter, but out of love she would allow her to contribute her small portion so that she could have a personal connection to the finished product. So the analogy comes full circle, with the mundane mirroring the transcendent in a profound but accessible way.[4]

Such is our whole theme of imaging the Church, and such is the privilege of nourishing souls. Returning to our point of the mutual exchange of gifts at a meal, we might see a variety of offerings: a gift of food or drink to be shared at table, rich conversation, a festive mood, a particular way of showing gratitude and, it is hoped, laughter and added joy. Yet if we are giving with the generosity of God, we cannot make claims on the other or demand a particular reaction; we must receive each guest as he or she is. In a family setting it is each of our family members and their unique personalities that will truly create memorable meals.

What women often focus on is the presentation of the meal, and this is important, though not the most important. We should make the setting and the food as attractive as possible, and good manners will add to the atmosphere. We would do well here to remember that all of etiquette is to be based on charity— love of the other—and not to be a form of elitism. Thus as we form our children, we do so out of love in order to prepare them to be more easily received by us and by others. Basic courtesy leads to the ability to join in the intimacy of the meal and truly delight in one another.[5]

Saint Clare, a religious of the thirteenth century, provides a beautiful witness to the link between the earthly meal and the heavenly banquet. Having come from a distinguished family with ample food and drink, she carried her spirit of generosity into her life of austere poverty. She knew the meaning of shared sustenance and its reflection of supernatural realities, and most importantly, she understood that all of creation is a gift to be handed on without measure or discrimination. There was no ego in her provision for others and no limit to her denial of self.

Clare trusted that God, as good and generous as He is, would provide. Indeed, so sturdy was her faith that He worked miracles through her and fed many with seemingly little food—the proverbial "loaves and fishes" story revisited as He fed His little flock of Poor Clares and their companions.

We must imitate Clare's trust, her generosity and her love of authentic communion so that more souls are pointed to the truth and wealth of the Eucharist. Christ waits to receive us with the gift of Himself, and the task of women is to live out in a variety of ways this sacrament that ultimately sustains us all.

CONFIRMATION

The sacrament of confirmation completes the work of grace God began in us in baptism. Confirmation is necessary to bring faith to maturity, and it provides in greater measure gifts of the Holy Spirit: wisdom, piety, counsel, courage, knowledge, understanding and fear of the Lord. As these gifts unfold and combine, we can see the rich potential of the human person. These gifts prepare the believer for all dimensions of life.

On the human level women can mirror this sacrament and enhance the people they encounter in a very tangible way. The verb *confirm*, at face value, means "to establish the validity of, to make firmer, strengthen, ratify."[6] If we apply this concept to the human person, it is evident that it is an act of both charity and truth to confirm all those we meet. This confirmation is an intrinsic part of womanhood. It is an act of truth to acknowledge the dignity of every person—his or her right to exist, to receive respect and to exercise authentic freedoms. What compels us to confirm others in this truth is our genuine love for souls and our trust that each has latent treasures within to be nourished for the greater glory of God.

To bring this to the practical level, we can consider the limitless ways that a mother can confirm her children through her natural interest in their growth, her desire for their holiness and her recognition of their inherent dignity and unique gifts. Without fawning or gushing false praise, a mother has the graces from her own sacramental life to wisely foster the good and to form her children in virtue. It begins with the initial eye contact—that mother-infant bond that wraps two souls in their own love affair and creates for the child the fundamental palette of positive human relationships. The mother subsequently follows the child's development at each turn with appropriate feedback. In a healthy family this will continue until death.

Key to the way that mothers confirm their children is allowing them to mature and grow. The mother's management of details and the course of events will gradually diminish, allowing children to blossom as independent adults. As this process unfolds, her confirmation transforms into acknowledgment of the child's freedom with continual encouragement through positive feedback. Here again is the opportunity to call on our feminine genius in order to maintain our standards while encouraging all that can be praised.

Sometimes the mother's task is to remind the child of dormant talents, previous successes or happy memories. She calls to mind his or her "better angel." Yet prayer and prudence are the best guides for how to bring out the good in each person.

Men too have to confirm others in their own way; in fact, the vocation of fathers to confirm their children is critical. An important dimension of the father-child relationship is the mother's responsibility, as primary receiver and caregiver of new life, to invite the father in and to allow him room to live out his fatherly vocation. This should begin even before the birth of children, as the wife confirms her husband in his manhood and in his efforts to protect and provide for them as a couple. As the family grows and the father proceeds to build relationships with his children, she lays the foundation for prudent, positive and encouraging exchanges.

Without the mother's blessing and cooperation, it is difficult or even impossible for children to receive their father's confirming words and actions, which are essential to the wholesome formation of both boys and girls. It should go without saying that a wife would never engage in the belittling of men, which is a staple of humor in many venues. We cannot countenance such jokes in our circle of friends, nor allow male-bashing comedy to entertain our children, nor let derogatory comments pass in our presence. The men in our lives must know of our esteem, for our confirmation reaffirms them in their essential vocation to care effectively for their families.

Family life is sloppy and complicated, we must admit. Every family deals with a critical dynamic in the recognition of the individuality of each member and the expectations of the rest. With prayer and wisdom—and a priority on discerning God's call to each soul—we can achieve a balance based on love and the proper respect for the legitimate choices we are all called to make. Bringing the supernatural dimension to this act of confirmation can be very helpful and freeing to the woman who struggles with the individuality of each child and the unique path God calls him or her to follow.

One elderly woman recalled her frustration with her mother over the different, seemingly unfair treatment given to two of her brothers. Her mother had responded to this angst by asking the daughter to hold one hand up and notice the difference in the fingers. The mother knew that her children's different personalities and needs required different responses. It was not a question of justice but of responsive love. Such was her reason for treating the two boys differently.

Pope John Paul II pointed out that the gift of motherhood that women enjoy "gives rise to an attitude toward human beings—not only towards her own child, but every human being—which profoundly marks her personality."[7] Beyond the mother-child relationship, all women have a distinct call to confirm the human person at every opportunity, to introduce all souls to this characteristic of the Church. Just as the Church cannot turn away those legitimately seeking the sacraments, there is no class or segment of individuals whom any woman can exclude from her charity.

Women religious are magnificent sources of confirmation to many, since the way that they channel their spiritual motherhood frees them to be available to the world at large. How many nursing homes are blessed with cheerful nuns who spread supernatural charity in their wake? How many sisters have been available to children in times and areas where mothers otherwise occupied could not be? How many orders have written their very constitutions around the need to build up the body of Christ one soul at a time, in creative and diverse ways?

As confirmation builds on baptism, the human act of confirmation builds on the hospitality and welcome already inherent in the woman's reflection of baptism. In essence the room is clean, the door has been opened and now the eye contact, respectful words and uplifting follow. This can envelop a neighbor's child, a coworker, a shop clerk or a student. Personalities and circumstance will determine whether a pat on the hand, a caress of the cheek or an embrace is appropriate. What is important is that the woman discern the needs of the other and step in to convert the time together into an encounter with the very love of God.

Imitating the Church's mission of confirming souls is a gift that women are required to share. Even as it may come more easily to some than to others, so also the methods will vary widely. Some have a way with soft words; others know that acts of love (even tough love) or a simple exchange will do just fine. The key is serving "the other," recognizing his or her need to be lifted up and strengthened. If we discover that our own woundedness or lack of role models inhibits our abilities, this simply means that we have to heal and form ourselves by finding the right examples to imitate.

Saint Katharine Drexel is a beautiful example of a woman who saw the dignity of those less valued by society and dedicated her life to loving God through them. Born in Philadelphia in 1858 to tremendous wealth, she responded to God's call to embrace poverty and work, predominantly with the Native American and African American populations of the United

States. She and the other members of the community she founded, the Sisters of the Blessed Sacrament, established institutions throughout the country. Their apostolates not only catechized and educated countless souls but also concretized her personal regard for the culture and heritage of these peoples. In other words, she confirmed the fact that all are equal heirs to the kingdom.

In this regard it is to be noted that the Catholic Church has long been distinguished for her efforts to uplift the individual and honor his or her culture, inasmuch as the details of culture can be combined with the deposit of faith. Natural law and all that is good in the human heart have been at the foundation of many diverse and rich traditions, which only need to be baptized and brought into the beautiful tapestry of Holy Mother Church. If some missionaries in the past have suppressed legitimate aspects of the cultures they encountered and imposed alien practices on unsuspecting peoples, this came not from the gospel itself but from a failure to understand and share the gospel properly.[8]

What is essential is to imitate the Church in her great desire to confirm what Christ her Spouse has planted in the hearts of His creatures, who only wait to know their Creator.

Mirroring the Sacraments of Healing

When man turned his back on God, it broke the Father's heart. Although He had to allow the consequences to mark humanity forever after, in His mercy God wanted to offer as many avenues as possible to bring man back to wholeness. Grace abounds throughout the world—flowing from the side of the resurrected Lord—but is particularly available in rich doses through the sacraments of healing: reconciliation (or confession) and the anointing of the sick. What these gifts of Holy Mother Church do in the realm of the supernatural, it follows that women shall excel in on the natural level, making manifest the divine embrace offered to the soul in need.

RECONCILIATION

When sin entered the world, relationships were damaged in two ways: We humans no longer could respond properly to the love of God, and we no longer could interact peacefully with one another. Since there are both vertical and horizontal dimensions to the sacrament of reconciliation, it follows that both dimensions are important to the vocation of women, who live out this sacrament in everyday life.

The natural solution to overcoming any sort of divide is to build a bridge, and women form such bridges of unity beautifully when they apply themselves to healing the rifts in relationships about them and bringing souls to God. Being sensitive to the needs of people, attentive to subtle messages and creative in setting up situations and personal encounters are all parts of the feminine genius that we can use for this important task.

We need prudence to know when to speak, when to remain silent, when to offer help and when to wait for a more opportune time, so that the one in need is capable of responding to the guidance offered. Prayer provides the greatest light in this effort. Each woman must be docile and prepared for her own growth and healing as she works for the unity of those around her.

VOCATION TO LOVE

Family life is rife with conflict, which can be managed for the most part only through grace. Living in close quarters magnifies the defects of each person, and charity often proves difficult. While it is incumbent on the involved parties to apologize and repair the damage that harsh words and rough actions bring about, women can do much to nudge along the apologies and soothe hurt feelings. As we go before the Lord daily, we ask for His wisdom in mending these little rifts, adding our personal sacrifices, which can go a long way toward softening hearts and reconciling wounded parties.

Unfortunately, not all conflicts are small. Many times they go beyond hurt feelings to outright grudges, resentments and even hatred. Often, we are offended by reproaches to ourselves, but we may feel just as keenly our loved ones' hurts from the actions, words or neglect of others. We can agonize over how to bring about unity once walls are thrown up; sometimes relationships appear unsalvageable. In such instances we have a glimpse into Christ's pain over disunity. We find ourselves linked to one of the keys of His Passion: our distance from God and our inability to live in His love.

The work of restoration through forgiveness and reconciliation is the province of the Church. She seeks to bring the Passion of her Bridegroom to all souls. The work is hard, often filled with suffering. It is only successful where those who love Christ bring His grace to those who need it.

We cannot neglect this important dimension of the Church we image—nor can we contribute to the task by our own refusal to forgive. The vulnerability of women to be hurt physically and emotionally would seem to inhibit their work of reconciliation, but it is not so. Love in a fallen world entails suffering, and the choice is stark: to love and risk the pain, or to withdraw and become cold. The latter is a frightening response but widespread, given the lack of faith in our world and the inability to understand that suffering can be linked with Christ's Passion and bear fruit for all. Suffering makes little sense in a secular world, yet the founding truth of our faith is that love bears all things for the beloved.

God reaches out to His children through those who would serve Him, and He walks with us through our trials, bearing our very suffering in His own body. We cannot allow our fears of what love may cost to keep us from loving. Nor can we allow our own scars and wounds to make us incapable of helping others who need to learn reconciliation. He who by His own example taught us to forgive offers us constant renewal in the sacrament and would have us pass along the divine gift. We must be free of our own resentments in order to see the needs of our neighbors.

A MODEL OF FORGIVENESS

One extraordinary example of a woman who sought to restore unity to the mystical body of Christ is a Russian woman, Irina Giorgi-Alberti, a writer who was an assistant to the famous author and dissident Alexander Solzhenitsyn during his many years of exile. Born in 1925, Irina was raised an Orthodox Christian and converted to the Roman Catholic Church.

Irina saw clearly that a twofold breach was destroying Russia: the decades of atheism imposed on the Soviet Union, wrenching its citizens from their proper relationship with God, and the crippling battle between the various Christian confessions in Russia, which pitted the few remaining believers against each other. Her countrymen were brimming with anger over injustices, violence and personal animosities within villages and across the vast nation. The suffering entailed broken families, exile and torture, betrayal and death.

In the last years of her life, Irina published a weekly newspaper and directed a Christian radio station—both efforts to bridge the gap between Catholic and Orthodox faithful. Realistic about the ways of the world, she recognized that "the desert of atheism that was dominant for 70 years can only disappear slowly. 'Who is this God of Whom you speak to us?' is a question often asked of us. And another is, 'Why do you call yourselves Christians if, while adoring the same God, you are divided among yourselves?'"

By special invitation Irina attended a Synod of Bishops for Europe in 1999. There she offered herself as mediator, carrying words of reconciliation from the Orthodox laity in Russia to Pope John Paul II. She turned to the pope and in an emotional tone said:

> Many in Russia, among those who have found Christ or who are sincerely seeking Him, have asked me to say not to accept the high-level political maneuvers as the true expression of their feelings. Above all they ask you to forgive them, not to abandon them, not to forget them, not to fall into the traps often set for you.... If this occurred, it would really be the end, for Russia in any case. If the end has not come, it is, I repeat, mostly due to Your Holiness, and in thename of those who know, I have been entrusted to tell you Holy Father: God will reward you hundredfold.[1]

Here is a woman who used the talents she was given and the circumstances of her life to be a true bridge of understanding and unity where sin had left a great, painful divide. Each woman can do the same in her own life as God wills, if she is willing to suffer the demands of love and forgiveness. In imitating the Church on a small scale, she can embrace her family, friends and coworkers as her own "mission territory." There she will pray, make sacrifices and work persistently to bring about authentic communion, so that we all may be one in Christ Jesus.

THE ANOINTING OF THE SICK

The anointing of the sick has had varied names throughout history, which have both helped and hindered its use in the Christian community. This important channel of grace for those in special need has both a spiritual and a physical dimension and should not be shunned out of misguided fears, especially fears concerning death. When it was referred to as extreme unction or the last rites, many denied themselves its graces and healing powers in the face of illness, assuming it was only for the time when death was imminent. Others, connecting its use with physical healings, missed its subtle and powerful graces for strengthening the spirit in the face of pain and suffering.

The *Catechism* notes that there are four dimensions to the reception of this sacrament, and each bears consideration for the woman who wishes to mirror them in her own life of service to the weak.

1. "The first grace of this sacrament is one of strengthening, peace and courage to overcome the difficulties that go with the condition of serious illness or the frailty of old age" (CCC, 1520).

2. There is the recognition that the infirmity is directly linked to the passion of Christ, which won for us the possibility of heaven (see CCC, 1521).

3. The reception of this sacrament reminds us also of the communion in which we all participate in the mystical body of Christ. Thus as we pray for the sick, the sick offer their sufferings for all, and the graces they receive in some way benefit the community at large (see CCC, 1522).

4. Finally, when this sacrament is given at the point of death, it imparts the necessary graces for the inevitable journey to the Father and brings to fullness the conformity to Christ begun in the anointing of baptism and strengthened by the oils at confirmation (see CCC, 1523).

WOMAN'S HEALING GIFTS

Women have been drawn to care for the sick from time immemorial. From vigilance over women in childbirth, to the care of newborns, followed by the attentiveness that mothers exercise in bringing children through the fragile years to adulthood, women have been skilled, by necessity, at reading the subtle and not so subtle signs of physical well-being. Until recently, extended families lived in close proximity, if not together, so the care of the elderly and frail was an additional dimension of the woman's vocation.

Nursing is a vocation that closely resembles what the Church offers to her people. Often, particular women stood out in their respective communities for giftedness in remedying various ills, and many depended upon their experience. Professionally, women have the opportunity to bring their compassion into hospitals, nursing homes, hospice care and even missionary clinics. These professionals are pursuing the work that religious orders established and carried out for many centuries, and respect for their work will always be profound.

Interestingly, Henry VIII's rejection of Roman authority over the Church in England in the sixteenth century, and the subsequent destruction of Catholic institutions, may have contributed to the dearth of skilled nurses in that country in the centuries that followed. Despite the widespread fame of Florence Nightingale (1820–1910) as a foundress of modern nursing, the truth is that she had to fight fiercely for access to her country's needy soldiers during the Crimean War. Military authorities were horrified at the thought of allowing women close to the front, although it was a long-standing tradition in Catholic countries to have nursing orders of sisters minister near battlefields. In strictly Protestant countries the absence of religious life for women—and the freedom such a vocation allowed—combined with the rejection of the sacrament of the sick may have meant that religious imagery and structures proved insufficient to foster this vocation in women.[2]

Even in modern societies, where husbands and wives, sons and daughters leave home to earn money, women still sense the need to be the primary decision-makers concerning the health care of their loved ones. Their responsibilities cover myriad familial relationships, from caring for sick children to welcoming aging relatives into the home for additional attention. They run the gamut from the Band-Aid and kiss for the scraped knee to the agony of watching a loved one die.

The ability to empathize with those who are suffering and the fortitude to work diligently for the good of the patient come easily to many women; other women can muster these abilities when love compels them to do what natural inclination might cause them to avoid. Some may grumble and cajole the men in their lives to be more attentive, but the natural feminine attachment to the human person causes her to take the lead in meeting the needs of the sick.

REACHING OUT TO HEAL

Taking the time to visit the sick is an act of charity and a corporal work of mercy, mirroring the Church's concern for the struggling soul. It provides a bridge between the wider Christian community and the infirm, who are often feeling isolated and forsaken in addition to living with pain or discomfort. The healing touch and gentle words of a thoughtful visitor reflect the anointing the Church offers sacramentally, and empathetic care is a visible manifestation of the spiritual consolation that accompanies the blessed oils.

Key to our image of the Church in this way is that the spiritual needs of the patient are always a consideration, and his or her eternal life is a factor in our approach. The vulnerability of the one who suffers often makes the attendant privy to information that she can wisely use for the good of the person's soul. Through loving insight and discretion, the caregiver may discover emotional burdens or anxieties that are preventing the person from embracing the cross and plumbing its rich meaning. With prayer and discernment she can offer counsel and wisdom, helping establish peace and focus the heart and mind more fully on God, as in the administration of the sacrament.

Rose Hawthorne Lathrop (1851–1926), a convert to the Catholic Church, felt deeply the call to serve those sick with cancer. In the nineteenth century this disease was thought to be contagious, so those suffering its effects often were cast out by their families. Rose studied this illness and learned what could be done for those afflicted with it. Then she set out to make a difference.

Rose worked alone at first, but gradually more and more young women who shared her desire to minister to the sick and dying joined her. Founding the Servants of Relief for Incurable Cancer, Rose opened several homes where cancer patients could come to live.

Sustained by her passionate love of Christ, Whom she recognized in those who were sick, and wisely combining it with a practical formation in nursing, she endured the trials of poverty, hard work and cantankerous patients, amid the difficulties of city life at that time, to make the final days of many people infinitely more peaceful than would have been possible otherwise. God, in His turn, blessed the work and showered it with the gifts and graces that allowed it to continue and grow.

The Servants were ultimately received into the Dominican Order, where they could live out the words of Saint Dominic: "We are to bring to those we serve the fruits of our contemplation." This focus links beautifully the spiritual and physical dimensions of healing. The Servants help their patients reflect on the supernatural meaning of suffering and the realities of death and resurrection.

A MATTER OF LIFE AND DEATH

The Church always has recognized the value of human life and taught clearly that suffering wins graces for the soul. Our lives and actions must reflect these truths as well. As we see society toying with euthanasia as a legitimate response to human suffering, our fidelity to the truth and constant witness to love in the most difficult of circumstances are critical to establishing a culture of life.

Surveys of the chronically ill show that depression and feelings of worthlessness assault them, leading some to want to end their lives. Being surrounded by ambivalent family members or those who cannot see the transcendent meaning of suffering only adds to their burden. At a time when the population is aging rapidly, it falls primarily to women to bring the compassion of the Lord to sickbeds, the love of Christ to the lonely and a defense of the human person into the dialogue about end-of-life issues. The Hail Mary, the prayer to our model mother, especially calls to mind the critical hour in our pilgrimage when we meet God. Women must spread the message of life and be present with this truth at the side of those who suffer.

Finally, we should take a moment to look at the way that women have cared for the dead. Burying the dead—also a corporal work of mercy—is the work of the Church. Knowing in life that the body is a temple of the Holy Spirit, we are taught to reverence it even when life has passed.

For countless centuries and in widely divergent cultures, women have given the care for mortal remains. This is a natural extension of God's initial entrustment of the person to the woman through motherhood. In death the body—after whatever length of struggle in this life—is given to her for her final maternal touch. Mary profoundly exemplified this: Christ was entrusted to her in infancy, and Tradition has Him passing through her hands between the cross and the grave, as Michelangelo's *Pietà* portrays.

From the Gospels we know that it was a group of women who went to the tomb to anoint Christ's body the day after the Passion. They brought costly spices for His burial, as was the custom in honoring the dead.

Such is the privilege of woman. In all of these circumstances—passing injuries, chronic illnesses, death and dying—she finds herself called to image the work of the Church. I pray that all women can persevere in this service, and that the gifts they offer to souls in Christ's name will be available in their own hours of need.

CHAPTER FOUR

Spousal Love

At the heart of each person's vocation, he or she is called to a deep communion with God and others. In this chapter we will turn our attention to the "social sacraments" of matrimony and holy orders, and then we will consider the consecrated life for women, which espouses them in a mystical way to Jesus Christ. In each of these settings, the nuptial backdrop to God's creation is manifest in a profound and tangible way, since all three give flesh to the covenantal, life-giving relationship between bride and Bridegroom.

Although the prime focus of this book is to help women understand their femininity and how that manifests itself in everyday life, women must also understand the vocation of men, with whom they build societies and share their lives. Since the essence of the woman's vocation is to image the bride, then it follows that the man's vocation will be to image the Bridegroom. Here we will look briefly at authentic masculinity in order to better appreciate the complementarity of the sexes within God's creation.

THE FOURFOLD REALM OF MASCULINITY

One of the psalms offers a short outline of the responsibilities of the bridegroom in a spousal relationship. The admonition to the bride at the outset calls us to attention: "Praise the LORD, O Jerusalem! Praise your God, O Zion!" (Psalm 147:12). What follows are the Lord's promises to His beloved: "For he strengthens the bars of your gates; / he blesses your sons within you. / He makes peace in your borders; / he fills you with the finest of the wheat" (Psalm 147:13–14).

What a gracious Lord Daughter Zion has, and what remarkable promises He gives to her in order to reveal His goodness and draw her praise! According to what is encapsulated in this short passage, we can depend on the Lord to protect us, to give us children, to grant us peace and to provide for our material needs.

God calls men to reflect God the Father, so we can hope for the same promises from them. The husband is to protect his wife, to father her children, to govern the home responsibly and to provide adequate sustenance for his family. Similarly the priest spiritually husbands the Church: he pastors those in his care, lovingly welcomes new members, preaches the truth in love and ministers the life-giving sacraments.

Although these promises seem to prescribe a fixed relationship, in actuality they leave great latitude for the woman. For example, when a husband "strengthens the bars of [her] gates," he does more than tend to his wife's "honey-do" list. A good husband takes responsibility for the family and the home in a way that allows his wife to live her vocation.

A husband does not cage his wife against her will or limit her mobility in any way. Gates are meant to open as well as close. The husband must keep them in working order, while the woman retains discretion on how to use them. Just knowing that the gates are strong and operative gives her a sense of security while allowing her the freedom to come and go, to welcome others or keep them at bay when necessary. Thus she can live the hospitality to which she is called, nurturing and tending to those who need her and yet limiting access when she or someone within prefers solitude.

As to the second promise, whether she is a wife or a consecrated soul, a woman's fruitfulness is a function of a man's fidelity and oblation. Husbands and priests make possible the graces of motherhood—the former within the domestic church, the latter for Holy Mother Church. God calls single women also to a gift of self through spiritual motherhood, and He empowers them for this through the sacraments they receive at the hands of priests as well as through the authentic fatherhood of the men in their lives.

In the third line, which is closely related to the first, we may wonder what "establishing peace in the borders" could encompass. As safe as a woman might feel with her gates securely fastened, the mere fact that evil prowls about in many forms is a cause for anxiety. Traditional night prayers remind the faithful that "[y]our adversary the devil prowls around like a roaring lion, seeking some one to devour" (1 Peter 5:8). For example, a mother's thoughts of her teen out on the road at night is enough to rattle her peace—only hearing the key in the lock sets her mind at rest.

A man who keeps evil at bay—by establishing rules for the safety of children, maintaining harmony with neighbors, making the legitimate needs of the family a priority—creates an outer layer of security that allows his wife greater peace of mind in her duties. Similarly, the priest must take authority over the evil one and teach his flock how to stand firm in the truth.

Of course, the woman also takes a hand in establishing harmony and building bridges of unity. In fact, her feminine genius is adept at creating structures of safety for her loved ones and beyond. Thus when the man fulfills his duty to establish the outer layer of security, she can work in concert with him, and together they enhance the safety of the most vulnerable in their care.

Finally, this passage acclaims the sustenance that men provide for women. More than simply "bringing home the bacon," men are called to generously provide to those in their care the very best that they can, including their time, attention, provision and support. As shepherds, they lead their loved ones with prayerful guidance, taking into account the details provided to them by the woman, who may be more attuned to the exact needs of the family. As protectors, men stand guard against threats to their livelihood and to the family's safety.

Men bear the mark of the Father-God, so much so that they risk blasphemy when they neglect or malign their masculinity. Women, for their part, must honor true masculinity, lovingly encourage its expression and respond with their own feminine gifts, so that the "finest wheat" God offers to everyone doesn't go unclaimed. With mutual respect and a real understanding of how both men and women cooperate within the family, children have a far better chance of understanding the abiding and unconditional love of God.

Courtship is the time to discern the compatibility of spouses. A man decides whether he can live side-by-side with a particular woman and whether she will help him to live a holy life. A woman does the same. One does not embrace a spouse with the intent of changing him or her; we know from abundant anecdotal evidence that this is a recipe for unhappiness. Peace under one roof presumes that the partners share the same mission and agree on how to achieve it.

THE ESSENCE OF FATHERHOOD

Just as the vocation of women is not primarily a list of things that need to be done but a habit of being, the vocation of fatherhood likewise should not be reduced to action, even service-oriented action. It is about "being," not "doing." Thus what the father *is*—an icon of God the Father—speaks to a truth.

The priest's primary responsibility is to spread the word of God—the seeds or *semina*—and he does it unto the spilling of his blood if necessary. His vocation is an invitation to partake of the priesthood of Christ, and he responds by doing what is required of him in that capacity. Likewise, a layman's visible and engaged presence to his wife and children speaks, relating the gospel in a personal setting, giving credence to the truths of God the Father. The fidelity of men to their vocations is a testament to all that is good and true pertaining to the promises of our heavenly Father.

Cardinal Joseph Ratzinger (now Pope Benedict XVI) said of the priesthood, "Being related to Christ means to be taken up into his existence as servant, and staying with him, at the service of the 'body,' that is, the Church. Precisely because the priest belongs to Christ, he belongs, in a thoroughly radical sense, to men. Otherwise, he would be unable to dedicate himself profoundly and absolutely to them."[1] These beautiful words can apply equally to fathers of families, who share a service to the bride in their own capacity.

What this proposes to men is that, ultimately, they should be reaching toward a transparency, in which their very being points to the word of God. There is a profound humility involved in masculinity. They hold their God-given authority and their varied realms of influence in trust for the Master. Just as John the Baptist spoke the message he was called to speak and then disappeared from view, the priest's "focus is not on himself but on the Other. Yet he is *vox*, voice, with all his being. It is his mission to become a voice for the word."[2]

The nuptial essence of this truth includes women, and therein lies our essential mission. Man is called to speak this truth with his very being, and yet *creation is in need of woman to give it flesh.*

Considering the varieties of spousal relationships in light of spiritual realities, each can add depth to the others to reveal the richness of the covenant God has made with His people. Far from the deist notion of a distant and disinterested God, our Creator has made Himself known as Father, Brother and

Spouse—all terms that indicate an interest and affection for each person that is intimate, familial and lasting.

Later we will delve into the covenant God established with the children of Abraham, indicating His burning desire for a relationship with the chosen people. For now we will turn our attention to the priesthood, the bond between husbands and wives, and religious life for women—each of which will tell us a great deal about God as Father and Bridegroom of our souls.

HOLY ORDERS

Those in holy orders—bishops, priests and deacons—are ordered toward service: toward teaching and leading and loving the bride of Christ, pouring out their lives in order to nourish and protect her. It has long been a discipline in the Western Church that priests choose to live celibately "for the sake of the kingdom of heaven" (CCC, 1579; Matthew 19:12). This primarily is an imitation of Christ the High Priest, but practically it allows priests to prioritize the needs of the Church, which could easily conflict with the legitimate needs of a family. Rather than thinking of priests as "single" men, it is more accurate to see them as spouses in a mystical union, providing the sacramental graces for the Church to be the fruitful mother she is called to be.

The priest himself needs to be vigilant that he does not consider his life that of a bachelor, which would be at odds with the sacrificial lifestyle that he should be living. The title *Father* is apt, since each priest lives in a state of wedlock with Holy Mother Church, and he is essential in providing spiritual seeds. The spiritual children that the priest and the Church together bring to heaven should be vast in number and rich in holiness.

It is true that women participate in the common priesthood, to which everyone in the Church is called, but not in holy orders. The difference between these priesthoods is explained in the *Catechism*: "While the common priesthood of the faithful is exercised by the unfolding of baptismal grace—a life of faith, hope, and charity, a life according to the Spirit—, the ministerial priesthood is at the service of the common priesthood. It is directed at the unfolding of the baptismal grace of all Christians. The ministerial priesthood is a *means* by which Christ unceasingly builds up and leads his Church" (CCC, 1547).

The *Catechism* further describes the essence of holy orders—the ministerial priesthood—as the call to imitate Christ in a tangible way, being "present to his Church as Head of his Body, Shepherd of his flock, high priest of the redemptive sacrifice, Teacher of Truth" (CCC, 1548). Interestingly enough, despite the fact that the priest offers aloud the prayers of the community and confects the Eucharistic sacrifice in the name of the whole Church, he is not configured to be a "delegate" of the people. Such a distinction would set him apart from the bride in an unacceptable way. Rather he offers prayer and sacrifices in union with the bride, the body of Christ.

At the same time he acts *in persona Christi*, as the conclusion of the Eucharistic Prayer epitomizes: *per ipsum, et cum ipso, et in ipso*—through Him, with Him and in Him. Thus the Head and the members of the body act in concert, as one body, to offer worship and sacrifice pleasing to the Lord—two in one flesh, as it were.[3] Any other interpretation would imply a wedge between the spouses that cannot exist.

HOLY MATRIMONY

This total union is what is at the heart of matrimony, "by which a man and a woman establish between themselves a partnership of the whole of life...by its nature ordered toward the good of the spouses and the procreation and education of offspring" (CCC, 1601). In this definition the parallel is clear between the work of the priest with his parish and the duties of husband and wife.

"The vocation to marriage is written in the very nature of

man and woman as they came from the hand of the Creator" (CCC, 1603). Men and women naturally yearn for one another for completion and satisfaction. Indeed, marriage has existed in one form or another throughout all times and cultures, and revelation has echoed its mystical qualities throughout salvation history.

In both holy orders and matrimony, it becomes abundantly clear that the vocation of woman is quite distinct from the vocation of man. The vocation of bride is ordered to that of bridegroom, equal to it in all dimensions, but not to be confused with it through an androgynous blurring of lines. The bridegroom protects his bride, makes her fruitful, completes her with his masculinity and provides the haven where she can prosper safely and comfortably. He gives that she might receive, and her receptivity gives life back to him and affirms his manhood. Together they guide the new life they have created toward heaven, cleaving to one another for support and sustenance unto death.

God was the first to reach out to man with a covenant. "You shall be my people, and I will be your God" (Ezekiel 36:28), He said to Abraham, establishing a relationship that would endure despite the infidelities of His spouse. "The nuptial covenant between God and his people Israel...prepared the way for the new and everlasting covenant in which the Son of God, by becoming incarnate and giving his life, has united to himself in a certain way all mankind saved by him, thus preparing for the 'wedding-feast of the Lamb'" (CCC, 1612; see Revelation 19:7).

The indissoluble nature of spousal love would be too much for fallen men and women to bear if holy orders and matrimony were not raised to the level of sacraments, with the graces commensurate with the demands of each. God, throughout history, has borne with sinful man through forgiveness and forbearance, teaching those who enter into these sacraments the way to persevere and succeed. With God all things are possible, even lifelong union, with all our defects and imperfections. "The entire Christian life bears the mark of the spousal love of Christ and the Church.... Christian marriage in its turn becomes an efficacious sign, the sacrament of the covenant of Christ and the Church. Since it signifies and communicates grace, marriage between baptized persons is a true sacrament of the New Covenant [cf. DS 1800; CIC, Can. 1055 § 2]" (CCC, 1617).[4]

Marriage is even considered the primordial sacrament, since in it is configured the entire relationship between God and man, and between man and woman. To this degree, imagine the graces that God would make available to those who attempt to live in such unions.

As a priest is consecrated to serve in a distinct way as minister, so husbands and wives are consecrated to one another, and the ceremonies involving both sacraments should be public and in the context of the Mass if at all possible. The prayers of the community help members properly discern their vocations before the vows, and these prayers provide an atmosphere conducive to fidelity once the vows are pronounced.

Marriage and holy orders rise and fall together; infidelity in one institution is echoed by unfaithfulness in the other. While this might indicate a possible death spiral for both institutions when marriages and family life become frayed and tattered, God provides the graces necessary for recovery if the community turns to Him in need and prays for His help. The sacrificial love of a few have prevailed on Him to restore spousal love to health in societies that seemed beyond the pale.

One who understood such sacrificial love was Elisabeth Leseur, a Catholic wife of a man named Felix, an ardent atheist. Although the life they led was far from satisfying to her—she lived her Christian simplicity despite her husband's animosity toward her faith and in the glare of Parisian high society at the turn of the twentieth century—she found peace in God through intense prayer and deep reflection. Showing the consolation that is possible when even one party to a marriage is spiritually whole, she offered her sufferings for the conversion of her husband. The combination of her sacrifices, her faithful witness and her diary, which Felix happened upon after her premature death in 1914, provided the grace for his reconciliation with Catholicism and eventual ordination to the priesthood.

What tremendous graces she had won for him, but also what an example she provided that he might understand the indissoluble nature of a covenant and how to cling to it for strength. While Felix had not understood these truths during her lifetime, it all became clear to him—both the fidelity of God to His promises and the ability for Elisabeth to love him unconditionally. One would speculate that his was a rich priesthood, built as it was on such a foundation of devoted love.

THE CONSECRATED SOUL AT THE SERVICE OF THE BRIDEGROOM

In the discussion of the sacraments of marriage and priestly ordination, I explained the nuptial meaning of the body in reference to the total gift of spouses—husband and wife, priest and Church—which accrues both special graces and new life. Spousal love is manifest in yet another way for Christians in the total gift of self through consecrated life. Although both men and women have lived this vocation in myriad forms and with different charisms since the earliest generations of the faithful, our interest will focus on women who make this choice in response to God's call.

Jesus refers to those who would make themselves eunuchs deliberately "for the sake of the kingdom of heaven." He says, "He who is able to receive this, let him receive it" (Matthew 19:12). Having elevated marriage to a sacrament and honoring a wedding feast with His first miracle, there is no doubt that

Jesus esteemed the love of husband and wife as good and holy. Some women, though, are called to an intimacy with God that precludes other relationships in order that they may manifest a strictly spiritual motherhood. These women, fully aware of the riches of married life, voluntarily renounce its benefits in order to answer a specific call from God, embracing poverty, chastity and obedience. In this way they offer themselves as an oblation or holocaust for Christ's mission.

As good as married love is, the Church has always taught that virginity for the sake of the kingdom is a higher good: "By the profession of the evangelical counsels *the characteristic features of Jesus*—the chaste, poor and obedient one—*are made constantly 'visible' in the midst of the world* and the eyes of the faithful are directed towards the mystery of the Kingdom of God already at work in history, even as it awaits its full realization in heaven."[5]

The first women in the Church to discern this unique call were Jewish, Roman and Greek virgins and widows who gathered in small communities. Consecrating themselves as "brides of Christ" to their local bishop, they lived especially sacrificial lives, renouncing many comforts and consolations in the expectation of rewards after death (see Matthew 19:29). For some orders the monastic uniform was designed to distinguish the women who renounced the world for Christ in this profound and complete way. Others chose clothing that would make them humbly blend into their surroundings, rather than stand out. Those in a cloistered life of prayer and penance for the people of the world wore the habit as a death to self, since they would no longer be visible to the outside world.[6] For all these women the spousal significance of their vocation was underscored by the fact that they "took the veil," which during the time of early Christianity was what married women did to set themselves apart from unmarried women.

Virginity is the highest good when offered to God. "This

means a life of partnership with Christ, marked by radiant joy, an obvious unselfishness, an inner peace which cannot be destroyed by any outer vicissitude, by the rapture with which one lives the Christian life."[7] Embracing total poverty, chastity and obedience creates a sign of contradiction for the eyes of the secular world. Thus the woman who answers this call becomes an eschatological sign—that is, a spiritual signpost that teaches those who encounter her and her way of life that there is another invisible reality. She is an *"image of the Heavenly Bride and of the life to come,* when the Church will at last fully live her love for Christ the Bridegroom."[8]

We cannot see these women as an extraordinary extension of the mystical body of Christ, as though their vocation has little to do with the average family or with the ordinary lay Christian. Rather, *"the consecrated life is at the very heart of the Church* as a decisive element for her mission, since it 'manifests the inner nature of the Christian calling' and the striving of the whole Church as Bride towards union with her one Spouse...[as] an intimate part of her life, her holiness and her mission."[9] And "the consecrated life, present in the Church from the beginning, can never fail to be one of her essential and characteristic elements, for it expresses her very nature."[10] Thus a study of this vocation would be instructive to all of the faithful who seek to understand the essence of Christianity.

A HARMONIOUS BALANCE

Fundamental to embracing Christ as Spouse is the need for "conversion, self-renunciation and compunction of heart,"[11] which each serve to make the soul receptive to the healing love that God offers. Silence, prayer, self-denial and love for the Eucharist feed the consecrated woman's soul. Then her private and communal meditation and study will help her to find a balance between her inner life and the external works that form the charism of her community.

Her prayer life will be structured around the word of God, which provides supernatural and life-bearing seeds; the sacrifice of the Mass, in which she renews her total oblation in union with the divine Victim; and the Liturgy of the Hours, which maintains communication between bride and Bridegroom throughout the day, much as a married couple keep in contact. The evangelical mission is to give flesh to the nuptial realities, since "there is a need for people able to show the fatherly face of God and the motherly face of the Church, people who spend their lives so that others can have life and hope."[12] Ultimately, these are the same threads that run through all the feminine vocations, uniting all the states of life!

In his apostolic exhortation *Vita Consecrata*, John Paul II centered much of his discussion around the Gospel account of the Transfiguration, which he later incorporated into the innovative luminous mysteries of the rosary. He reminded his readers of the words of Peter, "Lord, it is well that we are here" (Matthew 17:4), stressing that those words "eloquently express the *radical* nature of the vocation to the consecrated life: how good it is for us to be with you, to devote ourselves to you, to make you the one focus of our lives!"[13]

The Transfiguration indicates the purity of heart with which the consecrated soul adores her Lord. The love that any married woman feels for her husband should be magnified in the one who chooses Christ as spouse, or rather is chosen by Him. Rather than coming down off the mountain, she chooses to remain, soaking in the details of her beloved. "In the countenance of Jesus, the 'image of the invisible God' (*Col* 1:15) and the reflection of the Father's glory (cf. *Heb* 1:3), we glimpse the depths of an eternal and infinite love which is at the very root of our being."[14] Filled with the Holy Spirit, the bride of Christ says,

"You have seduced me, Yahweh, and I have let myself be seduced" (Jeremiah 20:7, *The Jerusalem Bible*). Her affectionate embrace takes her Beloved in His entirety: His beauty, His wisdom, His love for all creation *and* His suffering.

Her mission of love, filtered through the charism of the community she joins, will motivate her to serve Christ in a variety of settings. She may see Christ in the poor, the hungry or the neglected. She may serve Him through teaching, through tending the sick or elderly, through spiritual motherhood or through a life of prayer and penance. Other consecrated women undertake completely secular work—from publishing to engineering—that uses their talents and transforms their world in a unique way. Whatever the place and means of living their vocation, it is their vows that free them to be totally available to God's essential mission.

Our Lady is the paradigm of this vocation—in the words of John Paul II, "the *sublime example of perfect consecration,* since she belongs completely to God and is totally devoted to him."[15] Mary as virgin, bride and mother manifested perfect docility to the plan of God throughout her life, from the joy of the Annunciation to the sorrow of the cross and on to her triumphal coronation in heaven. "This virginal love is the source of a particular fruitfulness which fosters the birth and growth of divine life in people's hearts."[16]

This spiritual motherhood in which consecrated souls participate is entirely commensurate with the physical motherhood of married women, for they are part of the same nuptial reality of the plan of God. Love freely given unto death, without constraint, and ordered toward fecundity is a reflection of the divine life, which gives meaning and strength to holy orders, holy matrimony and consecrated life. Priests, married couples and the "brides of Christ" must rely on God and His channels of grace to find joy amid the trials of this life and to pursue the fruitful complementarity God intends.

Woman, living as bride in the midst of these mysteries, has a tremendous responsibility to be faithful to her calling so that the truth of God and his ways may be more accessible. The interplay among natural families, the priesthood and religious communities is constant and essential. The stronger each institution is, the greater the graces for all, and the more sure our path to heaven.

CHAPTER FIVE

The Church as Mother

Like many mothers, Ellen breastfeeds an infant who has allergic reactions to the food her mother eats. What this means is that Ellen must be extremely careful with her own diet, lest her child break out in a rash, become congested and be inconsolably fussy. For a woman who loves to cook and is known for clipping exotic recipes to try for parties, this infringement in her life would seem especially cruel. But Ellen is not fazed. Having waited so long for this child after suffering several miscarriages, she has gladly changed her lifestyle for the duration of her nursing months. Knowing the benefits of breast milk, she doesn't even entertain the possibility of weaning her child early.

Ellen gazes into the face of her daughter, who has just drifted off to sleep in her lap, and rejoices in this overwhelming gift. What are spicy chicken wings and soda compared to this precious gift of life entrusted to her? Plain cereal, rice, dry bread and cool water seem no sacrifice at all, when—truth be told—many women around the world would be grateful to have them in ready supply. She takes daily vitamins (without iron) and is allowed an occasional banana. Ellen knows that this is all so very temporary.

MOTHERHOOD: THE GIFT OF SELF

A successful lawyer, who had only one son from a marriage that failed, remarked to a friend that, when she looked back on her life, she was surprised to realize that the most important thing she had ever done was to become a mother. Many modern women lament that they realized only too late that more love and more life were possible. Rather than being a job wedged among other responsibilities, motherhood is a vocation—and a powerful calling at that, since it speaks to the essence of a woman's being.

While motherhood was part of God's plan from the beginning, when our first parents sinned and rejected the will of God for their lives, part of the punishment was the suffering that women would undergo in order to bear children. One can imagine women from every culture comparing their aches and worrying over unexpected pains attached to pregnancy. From morning sickness to heartburn, from stretch marks to back problems, mothers have shared many a detail, sending countless men scurrying from the room, cave, igloo or hut.

There is a certain consolation in sharing stories of suffering with someone who can relate to them personally. Such sharings also drive home the fact that there is an enormous physical cost attached to bringing new life into the world, a price no woman can escape. As God would have it, the pain is relative to the fruit, and what comes at such a cost has its overwhelming rewards.

Motherhood from the outset demands the total gift of self if it is to be done well. To live hospitality at this phase and to joyfully sacrifice one's own comforts is to begin to wrap the heart and mind around the Christ Child. It is an invitation to grow in the spirit of service and to live for others, even if only piecemeal.

Nancy sent a note to her dearest friend to announce that "I'm going to be somebody's mother!" That "somebody" should be embraced with a willing heart, thoughtful preparation and a commitment to live the months of gestation in such a way that the child has the best possible start in this world. It is the setting for the most intimate form of hospitality, the welcome of an honored guest.

Here and beyond we have a wide range of opportunities to enhance the lives of others so that they will be able to find God, love Him and one day enjoy life everlasting. This whole journey of oblation will be one of fits and starts, and in all honesty it may continue as such for decades. Opportunities to serve will present themselves around the clock in countless ways, sometimes tumbling over one another in rapid succession—confusing, overwhelming, almost suffocating.

Our gratitude for such a rich invitation ebbs with our energies and dissipates altogether on many days. Some opportunities will actually ring with success; others will reveal to us our shortcomings, self-absorption and frustrating attachment to sin.

God wants us to understand the supernatural reality into which we have been invited, the spiritual dimension of motherhood. Essential to this is remembering that it is the motherhood of the Church that we are striving to imitate. In each encounter between mother and child the woman should look to the larger model for how to act—and react. But more important than looking to the Church as a model, "the soul of every woman in the state of grace takes part in this motherhood."[1] The motherhood of the Church is *given flesh* in the lives of women!

The Church has nurtured her young for two millennia, and none other than the Holy Spirit has guided her expansive vocation, so we have real wisdom to draw upon and a concrete example that has weathered all storms. Just as the Church exists as a path to God the Father, mothers exist as bridges between children and truth. The truth is etched in children's hearts, but it is for the mother to draw it forth as God's gift.

It goes without saying that motherhood need not be physical. Beyond pregnancy and adoption within the family circle, all women are called to shower their motherhood on the world in the particular ways that God makes possible. The single woman, the barren wife, the widow and the consecrated bride of Christ will all be given opportunities to exercise motherly hospitality: to shelter others, to harbor the lost, to love the unmothered.

Consider Alice, who was orphaned at three months and adopted at age six by a dysfunctional couple. By the age of twenty-four she had separated herself from almost all family ties. Now she marvels at the spiritual mothering she received all through life, first from a distant aunt, then from an elderly neighbor who had no children, then from several caring women in her parish and ultimately from Christ's own mother, when she was ready to receive it.

Wisdom is available to those who beg God for it, and then the needs of others will become apparent. As long as Christ is the wellspring of love, a motherly gift of self will multiply one's energies and resources, rather than draining them. Recourse to the sacraments is vital, and the nourishment therein is sufficient for the vocation to which we are called.

LOVE WITHOUT STRINGS ATTACHED

Since the days of Cain and Abel, teenagers have provided a particular test for parents. Families often have to scramble to survive the adolescent years. One mother's reaction to a rebellious son is quite telling, and the lessons she learned are extremely valuable.

For several years Kenny had become increasingly sullen and resentful, until at age seventeen he was out of control. Despite a warm and loving home, grounding in the faith and moderate material advantages, this child pushed every limit, making an otherwise pleasant home miserable. Shouting matches took place, Kenny was physically rough with his siblings and his grades began to fail. The whole family would dissolve into tears at least weekly. Kenny's parents seriously considered asking him to leave, despite the fact that he hadn't finished high school.

Through prayer and counseling, Kenny's mother came to understand that her love had carried with it certain conditions: She welcomed his good behavior with joy and bristled with defensiveness at his irritating behavior. Fear had crept into her approach to Kenny, particularly the worry about his outward rejection of the faith. She made frequent comments to him and others about what he was doing to the family.

Now, all of these reactions are certainly understandable, given human nature and reasonable expectations within the family circle. But prayer showed this woman that she was not reflecting Holy Mother Church as she was called to do. Kenny was testing her and finding her love variable. Her behavior reflected her own moods as well as the circumstances Kenny posed.

She knew that was not how Christ loved her nor how the Church cared for her. She received constant generosity from Christ and His bride, despite her own unworthiness.

What is the Church to her children, especially the children who have strayed? Some Catholics haven't been to Mass since childhood, and others only go on major feasts or when visiting family members who still practice. If we imagine what their recollections of their early Church life might contain (theology aside), we would see light, reverence, dignity and—if we're of a certain age—a smell of incense. Most churches are beautiful in their own way, often containing images of Mary and other saints, symbols of Christ and—whether these Catholics know it or not—Christ Himself.

And common to all parishes of earlier years was an open door. No one questioned the right of anyone to come inside and participate. Just as the Church is always open and welcoming to each individual soul, so must our motherly hearts be open to receive our children, to quote from the ritual of the marriage rite, "in good times and in bad, in sickness and in health."

Kenny's mother realized that she had to respond with the constancy of the Church when it came to this difficult child. She must love him when he was unlovable, she must smile at him when her heart felt like breaking, and most of all, in those times when she felt he didn't deserve it, she must give the gift of herself to him. She realized that she had to mature quickly and love him firmly through it all.

Although the change was quiet and subtle—so subtle she didn't think Kenny would even notice—he began to react to her differently. She gave her "gifts" to him—clean laundry in his drawers, his room unexpectedly tidied now and then, favorite meals on his worst days—with no strings attached. She gave because she loved him. She loved him because he was in the image and likeness of God, despite his best efforts to distort that image. And most importantly, as part of that image, she respected Kenny's free will to take or reject the faith, to love the family or not and to choose his own path, which seemed to be leading so far from all she had imagined for him.

Kenny's mother only asked, in a calm moment weeks after her change of heart, that he return the respect as best he could. He did. Her boundaries and standards didn't change, but her heart did—and that's what made the difference.

Kenny is young, and there is no telling where he will end up in his life's journey. But what his mother realized is that she was responsible for offering to him what the Church offers to all of us: a sound education in the faith, a worldview complete with beauty, unconditional love, joy and a bridge to fatherhood both human and divine. The proposition of Christ as Savior is just that: a proposition. As God respects our free will, and as the Church honors the integrity of the individual, so must we reflect that truth and respect the free will of others, even our children, to either accept or reject that proposition.

The observation that "God has no grandchildren" is theologically valid. We cannot wield our parental authority as coercion in the faith, no matter how tempting it is to choose for our children. We evangelize them as we would evangelize anyone, and our proximity gives us no room to hide in our everyday witness.

It is telling that Kenny's demeanor changed paralleling the subtlety of the change in his mother. He responded to her cues and mustered the maturity to bring a measure of harmony into the home. Although he wasn't the "model child" she had envisioned (which may reveal in her a form of idolatry), now he was free. As his mother removed the invisible shackles of what she had mistakenly called love, the effects rippled through the entire family.

CREATING THE VISION

This mother learned a great deal about love, especially the motherly love of the Church and of Mary, the Mother of God. She learned that motherly hearts give love for no other reason than the fact that each soul deserves nothing less. The Church loves because she is commissioned to mother all souls and provide a safe haven, which will point them toward heaven. Mary loves because she is close to Christ and, with her unsullied heart, loves each person as she loved Him. We are, after all, His brothers and sisters.

This vocation to love caused Mary's own heart to be pierced by sorrow. When Christ asked her to mother His flock, she accepted the premise that bearing children would be painful. She embraces that motherhood and drinks from her chalice of suffering in imitation of her Son. Such is motherhood for all women, because life is costly.

An important part of motherhood is its ability to bring out the beauty of souls, fostering their capacity to love and receive love in return. It begins with the woman's attention to the phys-ical needs of others, taking into account both their basic require-ments and their unique affections and desires. Scripture reminds us of this practical stepping stone in evangelization: "If a brother or sister is ill-clad and in lack of daily food, and one of you says to them, 'Go in peace, be warmed and filled,' without giving them the things needed for the body, what does it profit?" (James 2:15–16).

A thoughtful woman can remember a variety of details, such as "This child prefers this dessert," "He likes to do this," and, "I'll wash this sweater since she'd like it for her class party." I know of one dear woman who knew of her only granddaughter's love for a particular icing. Before each visit she would deliberately make a little more than her cake would require and leave it in a cup in the refrigerator. After kisses and greetings the little girl would race to the fridge to find her treat. It wasn't until she tried the recipe herself years later that she realized how much work had gone into that little gesture.

Such details go beyond mere food and clothing, allowing each personal encounter to be one of grace and charity. After a child receives love and affirmation—which is the rightful response to every human person—he or she can in turn offer it to others, building a communion of souls based on authentic values. The subsequent fruitfulness born from one thoughtful gesture of love knows no bounds, as God can multiply it beyond our imaginations.

A MOTHER CREATES A BRIDGE TO THE WORLD

Motherhood and the vocation to teach are intricately related, since a mother serves as the integral bridge to realities both mundane and supernatural. When the human person is received with dignity, his or her criteria for behavior are based on virtue and truth, enabling growth in holiness. A mother who nurtures well can reveal to her child the world beyond, beginning with an introduction to the father, to God the Father and then to various forms of reliable and just authority. This enhances the child's understanding of the hierarchy of the universe and its order. A spiritually whole mother can present truth, goodness and beauty in the simplest of ways, which will turn the child's mind to the reason for his or her existence and to the appropriate response to other people and the things of this earth.

In contrast to the well-formed mother, a woman with anger, resentment, bitterness or dysfunction can give her child a distorted view of God, other people and the created universe. Her confusion and pain will color the world of those she influences and make their integration with this world more difficult. In particular, if she misunderstands the hierarchy God has created, has been hurt by men or has never been mothered herself, she will experience difficulty in conveying the love and understanding that are rightfully due the child. Rather than showing the way to God the Father and the child's earthly father on healthy terms, the abuse of authority and her own pain can incite her to tear down patriarchy, an offense that we have linked to blasphemy itself.

Motherhood and fatherhood are entwined and essential to each other. Without fatherhood a woman is not a mother. How tragic that many use their influence to tear down the very thing that entrusts to their care the human person. While recognizing the wounds that lead to this mind-set, we must pray for the unhealthy mother and reject the devastation that her worldview creates. The motherhood of the Church accomplishes this.

There are many dimensions to the image of Holy Mother Church. Beyond the examples given in earlier chapters on the sacraments, the Church offers formation, catechesis, a means to holiness, a life of order, a haven of peace and a source of grace. After each encounter with the sacraments, the words of the priest bid us to go forth and bear life and grace into the world, which neither knows nor understands them.

Is it any wonder that we need to rush back to our Mother Church often? Weekly, daily, sometimes hourly, we cling to her and the comfort she provides in a hostile and fallen world. As a youngster sets forth in his little world—perhaps a backyard or a neighborhood—he touches base often with his mother for sustenance, an occasional bandage or a word of encouragement. And so it continues, with the daughter away at college suffering a breakup, with the married son concerned over his first child's fever, with a grown child on a lonely business trip. All have the need to "check in with Mom." The mother embraces all, carrying them in loving arms to their Father, who loves them even more than she does. Thus she witnesses to the unfailing love between the Bridegroom and His bride.

MARKETING MOTHERHOOD

Where is motherhood now? Interestingly, in our capitalist world motherhood has been kept alive through constant demand, though it's shredded and rewrapped in unrecognizable forms. It is to be found in the fresh sheets turned down nightly at the upscale hotel; in the carefully folded linen napkins at fine restaurants; in the day-care provider's songs and stories; in the books stocking the self-help aisles at the local bookstore, whose titles shout "girlfriend" intimacy and affirmation; in the attentive smiles of imported nannies and the patience of high-priced au pairs; in the sincere faces of talk-show personalities who ask to hear that woeful tale one more time; in the glossy pages of magazines dedicated to passing along recipes and household hints; in wise psychologists with one eye discreetly on the clock; in school nurses who dry tears and comfort bewildered children; and in countless other venues providing flashes of affection on the company dime.

Remarkably, motherhood sells, though we would be loathe to peddle it by that name. It is a simple fact that impersonal service is unacceptable, and consumers want the kind of interaction that acknowledges their dignity. A cool sales clerk or an abrupt customer service exchange will be referred to a supervisor, and heads will roll. Courtesy is essential in the business world, but the products in demand are often the details of love that a mother traditionally offers in the home, if she is present.

Employers have struck gold in the rank and file of immigrant women, often hailing from Catholic countries rich in warmth and familial affection. Their diligence supports the work ethic that is essential to serving the public, and this is complemented by the wholehearted personal touch they learned from their mothers, who sent them off with tears and heartache in exchange for a much-needed monthly check.

It is essential that we respect the full weight of Catholic teaching concerning the rights of workers and the responsibilities of employers when considering the value of this "commodity." It is often the case that the unscrupulous take advantage of conscientious workers, and the seemingly simple work of less educated employees is not appreciated for the basic goodness of God that it mirrors. One day we may owe these diligent souls our very survival. They may be the ones to soothe mankind at a critical juncture.

MOTHER MARY, PERFECT IMAGE OF THE CHURCH

Mary is the first fruit and the most perfect image of the Church. Truly, she is the pilgrim who walks before us, the perfect follower of Christ and the model of faith we should all revere. But more specifically she is the archetype of bride and mother who teaches all women how to live authentic femininity. From her acceptance of God's plan at the Annunciation to her Assumption, she exemplified receptivity to the Father in a way that was life-giving and grace-filled for her and all who know her.

In a communion of Persons, as she was overshadowed by the Holy Spirit, she conceived the Man-God, and the eternal Word took flesh in a way that would have been impossible without her feminine cooperation. How could God "pitch His tent among us" without her immaculate womb, and how could God's fatherhood become manifest without her motherhood? The Incarnation will remain a mystery, but its spousal reality gives us an insight into the ways of the universe.

In an out-of-the-way corner of the earth, Mary provided sanctuary and hospitality to the Child who would lay down His life for mankind. She filled His home with warmth, nursed Him, sang to Him and, in union with Joseph, offered Him to the heavenly Father in the temple for the sake of the Law. She introduced Him to the world, taught Him speech and manners and loved Him with a perfect mother's love. It is the same love she offers to each of us, and it is the same love she wishes all of us to bear to the world.

Mary knew hardships—childbirth in a strange town, flight from danger into a foreign country, the loss of her husband, the death of her Son, the jeers of a hostile crowd thrown at the mother of a common criminal. His Passion wrought salvation out of disaster, and there she stood, clinging to this tree in docility to the plan of God, undoing the harm that our first mother had wrought.

Pope John Paul II reminds us that "this 'new motherhood of Mary,' generated by faith, is the fruit of the 'new' love which came to definitive maturity in her at the foot of the Cross, through her sharing in the redemptive love of her Son."[2] She felt His pangs of suffering with every fiber of her being, yet she harbored no bitterness. To the contrary, she embraced the fallen crowd to her motherly heart at the height of tragedy and later faithfully nurtured the fledgling Church.

How overjoyed Mary must have been to meet once again her heavenly Spouse at Pentecost, decades after His first embrace in Nazareth. He whose very breath had spoken the Word to her brought thousands to the feast after that first novena. The Spirit she had known in her inmost being was now showering her children in faith with life-giving joy, so that the family could grow in the communion of love.

She would always be mother to this band, offering the same love to each brother and sister of her Son, bridging the divide between the perfect Father and His wayward children. She intercedes for each of us as any mother would, wanting the best, offering herself for our salvation and, knowing the ways of children, forgiving the thoughtlessness of each.

Mary's intimacy with each member of the Trinity gives her sway and tips the scales of mercy on behalf of all who call upon her. She is present at every Mass, when the Holy Spirit through the *epiclesis* is summoned to embrace once again the bride in order to make Christ present. As obedient daughter, fruitful spouse and beloved mother, Mary holds a place in heaven beyond comparison; she is rightfully called Queen of the Universe. Her queenship is a feminine thing, a motherly honor and a boast for all women, for it is by her womanhood that God could reach mankind and bridge heaven and earth. As the Second Vatican Council teaches, "This maternity of Mary in the order of grace...will last without interruption until the eternal fulfillment of all the elect."[3]

Just as motherhood is a fixed and essential reality of the supernatural order, so must we do all we can to protect and foster it in the healthiest way possible for the good of all. Women, imitating Mary's holy boldness in stepping on the serpent who would strike her Child, should act with courage to counter his attacks on the powerful essence of their being. All women, whether single, married or consecrated, should establish the motherhood of Mary and the image of the Church as the foundations of their lives. The life of the world depends on it.

CHAPTER SIX

The Church as Teacher

To wrap one's mind around the history of education is impossible, but certain elements of teaching are pertinent to our thoughts on women. Obviously there are informal arenas of learning and more formal settings, ranging from instructing a toddler how to tie his shoes to granting Ph.D.s in prestigious academies. To consider the ways that women teach is to look at all of these places, building on the premises that motherhood is both physical and spiritual and that teaching is inherent to motherhood in all its manifestations.

Consider the affectionate term given to a beloved school from which one graduates, *alma mater*, which means "sweet mother." This phrase ties the two vocations neatly into one.

The teaching vocation belongs to more than those who train for it professionally; it encompasses all who are entrusted with guiding others toward the truth. That said, it would benefit us to look first at some recent scientific discoveries that have backed up some grassroots theories on the particular affinity women have for this vocation.

SOME SCIENTIFIC EVIDENCE

In the realm of biology, great advances have been made in the study of the human brain. Interestingly, while men's brains are slightly larger than women's, women have more dentritic connections between both the brain cells and the two hemispheres of the brain. Women have a strong capacity to transfer data from one side of the brain to the other, leading them to use both sides in an integrated way, while men operate more often from the left side.

The left side of the brain hosts myriad pieces of essential information, including language, complex voluntary movements, verbal memory, speech, reading, writing and arithmetic. Female brains, in general, are more adept than male brains at adding to these thought processes the information stored in the right half of the brain.[1]

It is the increased ability to access this right lobe that makes women distinct from men in the way they think. The right side of the brain holds the key to many areas where women seem to have an edge: for example, recognizing faces, reading facial expressions, picking up social cues, discerning objects by touch, nonverbal memory, spatial relationships, a sense of direction, the sense of smell and the overall integration of information.

Women's brains also have been shown to have a larger limbic area, the seat of emotion. Women tend to have a greater ability to feel emotion, and their enhanced language skills allow them to express it. They have a greater ability to bond with other persons, especially through their capacity to interpret nonverbal signs and signals. Throughout history women have been the primary caregivers for children.

Whatever the individual deviations are from these norms, medical studies have proven that the brains of men and women are different and cause them to have different overall strengths and weaknesses. Despite radical feminism's attempts to repattern the way that men and women act—insisting that their behavior is socially or culturally conditioned—we have to conclude that men and women are "wired" differently and that God planned it that way for His purposes.

What this has to do with education is subtle but essential.

While men may be content to look at data or impersonal facts to see their way to a solution, women more often use personal experience and intangibles as well as quantifiable evidence to create a more integrated, multidimensional picture. They may or may not be able to explain themselves to the men around them, but I'd like to think that this, too, is a part of what Pope John Paul II affirmed as "the feminine genius."[2] It is important not to deduce from this that women are better than men, or smarter or "superiorly wired"; they are simply different. Because of this difference the Church has promoted the understanding of "complementarity" between the sexes, which we are to receive as a good, for it is what God intended.

TAKING A HISTORICAL LOOK

Male-female differences have had important effects on the history of educational institutions in the life of the Church. After the fall of the Roman Empire, monasticism was the quiet force that restored order to Europe. One element that grew from this was a system of education built on monastic and, later, cathedral schools, which evolved slowly into a very structured way of passing along a sophisticated body of knowledge.

Families sent their young boys who showed academic promise to the monks to be educated. Families with money and the inclination sent their young girls to convents to be taught. The Church was guardian and dispenser of education, which integrated a variety of disciplines—rudimentary science, rhetoric, logic and elementary math—with a Christian worldview. In a simple and straightforward way, contemplative reflection was combined with intellectual inquiry, giving students a well-rounded education.

As the Middle Ages progressed, academic disciplines became more sophisticated. Teachers formed guilds, just as other workers of the age did. There was great pride in one's profession, and teachers were as inclined as other workers to show marks of distinction and to look out for one another in a Christian and brotherly way.

Cathedral schools competed for honors and fought for the better students. These schools evolved into the universities that we recognize even to the present day. There should be a great sense of satisfaction in the part that the Church played in seeking out knowledge of the world and making education available to a widespread portion of the population.

Unfortunately, two rifts grew that would prove to have serious negative consequences on the integrated knowledge that had served the Church and the world so well. There was eventually a split in academia between theology and philosophy, which ultimately mandated that students choose one or the other as a primary discipline. This breach was so pronounced that by the end of the thirteenth century, the University of Paris mandated that theological topics not even be discussed by those who taught philosophy.[3] Clearly the integration that had served education so well was being overcome by compartmentalization, as the universities drifted from their contemplative roots.

The second rift happened at roughly the same time, when women were refused access to the universities. This was not so much an objective indictment of women as students but a shift in the way that men saw the academy. True to the spirit of the age, the guilds had evolved into chivalric outposts, and the ecclesial ranks reflected the orders of the knights that fought for truth and order in the secular world. Eventually the universities barred all students and masters who were not part of the clergy.

Concretely, then, by the end of the thirteenth century, the feminine presence was gone from academia, and the spiritual motherhood of the Church was severely constrained. The effect was twofold and wholly negative in the long run.

Primarily, women, who had built many of their abbeys into

powerful learning establishments, no longer had access to the best formation. At that time Hildegard of Bingen, a Benedictine abbess, was the most renowned female academic, and her fields of expertise were many. There were other women as well—a long and impressive list—who had worked side by side with men in the scriptoria reproducing religious texts, had studied in the universities and had written treatises on a wealth of subjects. This collaboration now—school by school—came to a crashing halt.

The second effect was more subtle but every bit as harmful to the field of learning. Not only did women no longer have the benefit of the best of education, but the schools no longer benefited by the presence of women and their integrated way of thinking. What women brought to academia then—and still do—is "the living experience of the truths of faith."[4] What followed, sadly, was a disintegration over the years on many levels.

The potential whole was divided into compartments, running the risk that the individual disciplines would die without the others. With the elimination of the direct contribution of women to the theological process, their monastic experience was excluded. Further, a tendency to divorce the public and the private realms of life and to restrict men and women to each respected realm was enforced more and more.

Father Francis Martin, professor of biblical theology at the John Paul II Institute for Studies on Marriage and Family, has written, "In terms of theology, this meant that women were not allowed to participate in the elaboration of the theological syntheses to which they could have brought important contributions. Their own faith experience suffered in turn because their lack of training inhibited them in expressing adequately what they were learning from the Holy Spirit."[5]

It must be remembered that, while women have the gifts of feminine discernment, integration of ideas and grounding in real life experience, they also need the discipline and contrast of masculinity to round out their experience. "It is not good that the man should be alone" (Genesis 2:18) cuts both ways. Education suffered in ways that are still visible today.

FEMININE GIFTS IN EDUCATION: MARIA MONTESSORI

Two women in the last century have offered groundbreaking work in the realm of education and have given us excellent tools to work with while imaging the Church as teacher.

Maria Montessori was born in 1870, and at the age of thirteen she entered a technical school in her native Italy. After several years of engineering studies, she concentrated on modern languages and natural science, then decided to pursue a medical degree. While she enjoyed the total support of her mother, her father was strongly opposed (though he stopped short of forbidding her pursuit). She was further deterred by the fact that many medical schools didn't admit women.

Maria persisted with a virtual end run, entering the University of Rome to study physics, math and natural science. With this degree in hand, she was accepted grudgingly into medical school, where she excelled despite the shock to the community. She was awarded her diploma in 1897 with remarkable scores, and she joined the staff of the same university a year later.

One of her responsibilities opened a whole new world for her and led to her work in teaching. She regularly visited asylums for the insane, which housed children who had been labeled "feebleminded." She gradually discerned that these children for the most part were thirsting for experience in the most basic sense. She returned to school to study neurology for clues in how to help them. Later, working with many families with young children, she developed her teaching methodology, which has been hailed as a pedagogical breakthrough on many levels.

One dimension of her approach is the integration of body and soul to transmit truth. Reflecting the scholastic principle that "nothing is in the intellect which was not first in the senses,"[6] Maria's use of materials, especially her sensory-rich, play-based way of learning through manipulatives, reinforced the link. "From the hands to the mind" is an expression repeated often in Montessori training,[7] and the resulting classrooms are delightful places for children.

Maria's thoughts on something as simple as a human hand are profound:

> The hand is in direct connection with man's soul, and not only with the individual's soul, but also with the different ways of life that men have adopted on the earth in different places and at different times. The skill of man's hand is bound up with the development of his mind, and in the light of history we see it connected with the development of civilization. The hands of man express his thought, and from the time of his first appearance upon the earth traces of his handiwork also appear in the records of history. Every great epoch of civilization has left its typical artifacts.[8]

Maria underscored the foundation linking children's initial curiosity about their surroundings and their potential creative genius, which can unfold if they are well directed. This incorporation of the senses mirrors the way that the Church herself has always taught, both within the liturgy and beyond. Signs and symbols permeate Catholicism, from water to incense to bells—all of which stimulate the senses. And tangibles such as rosaries and processions, standing and kneeling, all bear sacramental meaning to the faithful. So in pondering this way of teaching, one sees a rich exchange, in which the Church offers the truths of God through the physical realities of His creation, to which the grateful soul responds with creations of its own, some of which become lasting cultural treasures.

From E. Mortimer Standing, a colleague of Maria's, came the accolade, "Many others have loved children, worked for them, and with them; but no one—since Our Lord spoke those startling words of appreciation of children to His generation—no one has so completely understood the soul of the child in its depth and greatness, in its immense potentialities, and in the mysterious laws of its development."[9]

The maternal doctor laid remarkable groundwork that enabled educators to serve the individual in a profoundly Catholic way. In her own words we find the essence of the teaching vocation:

> If we discover these laws governing the development of the child, then we discover the spirit and wisdom of God who is at work within the child. We must respect the objective needs of the child as something which God himself has instructed us to satisfy. This is the true spirit of education, for it means that divine wisdom itself is embodied through the actions of teachers and educators. If in the voice of nature we recognized the voice of God telling us to help the child, then we shall always be prepared to fulfill these needs. We shall then realize that in this way we are lending ourselves to God's plans and that we have a part in God's work in the child. We shall not then consider it a tiresome obligation selflessly to accommodate the demands of the child who is entrusted to our care, but shall see it as fulfilling the wishes of God, who reveals himself in the child. Only the recognition of God in his laws and in the expression of his will in children actually enables us to live for the child and to renounce ourselves.[10]

Thus, "as the eyes of servants look to the hand of their master" (Psalm 123:2), so the teacher sees herself in humble service to "the other," motivated by love to perform the tasks by which both will discover God's will. It is the concept of "unfolding" that describes what Maria saw in the natural development of a child, as he or she seeks to know the surrounding world and establish with it a give-and-take that will last a lifetime. In this approach the teacher simply provides an environment in which a child can thrive and reveal—or unfold—his God-given personality and gifts.

AND EDITH STEIN

Another woman used this very concept of "unfolding" in her work in education. This was in a different setting but nourished by the same faith.

Edith Stein was born into a Jewish family in Breslau, Germany, in 1891, roughly a generation after Maria Montessori. She was a lively and fun-loving girl, embraced by a loving family and a wide circle of friends. She proved a brilliant student, finally settling on philosophy as her field of study.

Despite the strong faith of her mother, Edith slipped away from the observance of Judaism. Intrigued by the witness of Christian friends and then captivated by the biography of Saint Teresa of Avila, she entered the Catholic Church at the age of twenty-nine. This not only transformed her life but also added immeasurable richness to her philosophical studies, especially to her understanding of the human person.

Edith completed her doctorate in 1916. Continuing her writing and lecturing extensively in German philosophical circles, she took a teaching position at a Catholic girls' high school. There she paid close attention to the nature of her students and the ways in which they learned. She was both disciplined and compassionate in her dealings with the girls.

Edith stayed at this post until 1931 and then took a position at the German Institute for Scientific Pedagogy. It was there that she established a system of education for women. She based her system on how women think, acknowledging the feminine gifts of integration of thought and service to the other, and on the nature of the person in light of God's truth. Further, she geared her methodology toward preparing young women realistically for the lives they were called to lead.

Edith insisted that the study of logic, grammar and languages can take woman's natural inclination for communication and use it for the good. This allowed God's gifts to unfold further and was thus in her eyes simply personality development. She also wanted women's intellects to be stimulated through study of the arts, humanities, mathematics, the natural sciences, logic and philosophy. It is obvious that she saw and understood the interconnection of the disciplines and the way that they formed a comprehensive means of understanding the world.

Her priority in the education of women was the understanding that women would be the ones to form the young through their motherhood and perhaps as professional teachers one day. Beyond this she saw no reason why women shouldn't pursue a wide range of professions, to the extent that they didn't neglect their children or lose their femininity. She hoped above all that her students would achieve self-mastery and confidence apart from the influence of others. One biographer paraphrases her as follows:

> You cannot achieve that self-containment of being, which is your excellence, if you live in a dependency on others for the fulfillment of your being. God alone can fully answer your need for love, and for that, He asks for your love. He also asks that we love others for His sake. If we love them for ourselves, we try to possess them and make use of them. What is needed instead is to strive for a wholeness of personhood ourselves and to help others to that same fullness of being.[11]

Reinforcing the point that woman's genius entails using her personal experiences to decipher God's will and to know herself better, Edith Stein used her wisdom to perfect her teaching methodology, aiming toward the "wholeness of personhood" in others. She recognized that empathy is the gift we use to know "the other." Through a woman's natural empathy, she can share consciousness with another in a way that creates a bridge of understanding.

GUIDING SOULS TOWARD TRUTH

Mothers and teachers create the havens of peace and tranquility that allow the soul to thrive and the personality to unfold according to God's plan. They perform similar work with those entrusted to them: They coax forth the good, introduce truth, embrace the needy and build confidence in conquering evil, all while striving to let go of the self. Imagine a world where each woman offers motherly wisdom and the guidance of a true teacher, where reality is grounded in authentic love and effective empathy, bridging the gap between what the eyes can see and what is left to faith.

A woman named Christina was pregnant with her fourth child. An OB-GYN nurse herself, she was still working part-time during this pregnancy, despite the fact that each of her previous pregnancies had ended with preterm labor. She was determined to avoid that outcome this time, disliking the complete bed rest it demanded as well as a drug that seemed to frazzle her nerves as much as it kept contractions at bay.

Although Christina paced herself and limited her exertions, the early contractions began. Knowing what her doctor's advice would be, she didn't tell him. She hoped to inch her way toward her due date, now six weeks away.

Finally she had to reveal her situation, and the doctor coaxed her to the hospital, slyly promising she would be home that very evening. As the hours progressed, the contractions intensified, and Christina thought of her responsibilities at home with the other three children. The inconvenience of it all blended with her feelings of failure to bring yet another pregnancy to full term. She knew she had been smug in organizing everything to make this one perfect.

A friend came to visit with a gift and a rosary, simply excited that the baby might be born on that day—of all days—the Feast of the Incarnation. She could see that Christina was struggling with her loss of control over the events in her life, just wanting to be home. She offered, "My sister, the nun, says that whenever you don't know what to do, you should do the most loving thing that you can for yourself."

Those words immediately cut through Christina's self-pity and pride. She submitted herself to the authority of the doctors for the safety of her child. She prayed the rosary and united her suffering and uncertainty with that of Our Lady. Her condition stabilized, and she managed to detain the arrival of her fourth child for a few more weeks.

Christina knew intellectually what was happening to her, and had it happened to one of her patients, she would have insisted that the woman put the health and safety of her child first. This was a time of blindness for her, she realized, because her pride had taken over. Although Christina was a wonderful mother and nurse, in this situation she was trying to control what was beyond her control. In order to truly serve the other, she had to become docile and allow events to unfold in God's time. The child in her womb was first of all His, entrusted to her. Christina realized that by being "super-mom" she was being no mother at all.

The lesson has served her well. Her children are thriving, and she is known in her community as an extraordinary mother and teacher. She has opened her embrace to far more souls than her own family, because of her ability to receive humbly from God and in turn selflessly offer her wisdom for the true good of others. Her growth in detachment from her own will is the same lesson that everyone has to learn, because only with this "surrender" of the self will one find perfection and authentic freedom, as Edith Stein believed so firmly.

This surrender was something that Edith Stein, in fact, exemplified. She willingly offered her very life in oblation for "her people," the Jews, of whom she would always be a part. After a decade of teaching in the world, she entered the Carmelite order in 1933 and joyfully embraced Christ as her Spouse. She continued her writing but could now nourish it with the contemplative silence for which she had thirsted for years.

In retribution for her bishop's letter of condemnation of Nazi policies in the Netherlands, which was read from the pulpits of all parish churches in 1941, all Jews—including Catholic converts—were rounded up and sent to Auschwitz. Edith was gassed immediately upon her arrival there—an educator slain for the heroic teaching of the Church, which she modeled with her life.

HUMILITY: THE CROWN OF MOTHERS AND TEACHERS

Both mothers and teachers excel when they respect the innate dignity of the persons entrusted to them. There are so many ways that our egos can become engaged, so that the path of the young ends up being a reflection of the woman who guides rather than of the glory of God. This is a natural temptation—both when things go well and when things go awry. It is so easy to look at a child or a student and attribute his successes to a particular teaching technique or the ability to communicate. Conversely, a woman might despair when her charges choose badly or fail to thrive.

Humility begs us to cling to Christ and remember that these souls are His. After making an honest assessment, and perhaps seeking trusted opinions about whether she has failed or could use another method to make her point, the woman must pray and sacrifice for the grace to bring things to right.

Women, sensitive as they are to what is happening around them, might also be tempted to look critically at other mothers and teachers and point out deficiencies or differences. When to speak and when to remain silent is one of the most difficult decisions, requiring heroic prudence to discern. A woman always must check her motives to be sure that they are based on love for others rather than on her own ego.

It is also important to remember that different children require different approaches. Perhaps God has provided the unique touch to another woman for a given situation. Prayer and patience will tell.

The last temptation we have to fight is that of overstepping the boundaries of authentic love. We know the importance of affirming those in our care and supporting their decisions in life. God gave each person the gift of free will, and a good mother or teacher guides the young in learning how to use the will wisely.

Often, sadly enough, our children or our students make mistakes or deviate from God's will in an obvious way. Sometimes they drift away from the Church, engage in the abuse of drugs or alcohol or cohabitate—to mention but a few of the unfortunate decisions children can make. These are painful situations in the life of a Catholic mother, and yet our response must combine love with truth or it is not authentic love.

PATIENT LOVE

Carla's son, Jeff, was always drawn toward God, and he never fought attending Mass even while a teenager. He established a prayer life and read the Bible on his own, which pleased both of his parents. While away at college, he joined a Bible study that was hosted by a nearby Baptist church, and he was swept up in the enthusiasm that surrounded the dynamic leader. He stuck with it for all four years and during that time fell further and further from the Church of his childhood.

Carla was heartbroken and more confused than ever when, in his senior year, Jeff brought home Sheila, a lovely Baptist girl, and announced their engagement. There was no doubt that the couple was to be married in the Baptist church and raise their family in that faith.

Jeff's parents sought the advice of a trusted priest, and then chose a course of action. Carla embraced her future daughter-in-law with the love of a mother. She met her where she was in her faith journey and offered all the support possible without compromising her own faith. She realized that, to this girl who may have had erroneous notions of what Catholics believe, Carla would be the only real example of the Church she would ever see. Carla set her heart on being quiet, loving, firm, open, welcoming, wise and patient.

When questions arose, Carla would answer them succinctly. When distortions were brought up, she would gently correct. Most importantly, she affirmed her daughter-in-law in her motherhood, at which she excelled. That affirmation, above all, served to bond the two women closely.

Time will tell if Jeff will bring his family to the Church, but Carla's unconditional love of her family members is the only authentic feminine response. Just like the Church that Jeff left, Carla's door is always open. Her heart beats in union with Christ, who awaits their coming more than she does. She waits patiently, bonded to her mother Mary in prayer.

This view of feminine love is a relief during times of trial, when we place the burden of concern at the foot of the cross where it belongs. Such is the vocation of mother; such is the Church that waits to embrace us all.

Women, in image of the bride, mother their children and teach them well, so that as their gifts unfold they will know the truth in all things and be capable of returning the embrace. Edith Stein wrote that "woman naturally seeks to embrace that which is living, personal, and whole. To cherish, guard, protect, nourish and advance growth is her natural, maternal yearning."[12]

Women must learn to give this total gift of self fully realizing that it may be spurned, misunderstood and unappreciated. How many women live in forgotten apartments, quiet rooms in nursing homes or deteriorating homes—waiting for letters, phone calls and visitors who never come. Some have raised families, taught or guided numerous children who have since wandered far in ingratitude.

These women, too, image the sad reality of the Church, who is spurned and abandoned. They must cling to the fact that there was heroic good in the gifts they gave. Christ knows their worth and their suffering. He caresses His bride, the Church, who shares His broken heart. The seeds He planted were watered with His blood. Women must open their eyes to the privilege of cooperating with Him in this task, and suffer with Him until the fruit is borne.

CHAPTER SEVEN

The Bride in the Old Testament

If our spiritual mother, the Church, manifests a real and significant part of the nuptial reality and is the authentic model for all women, then it makes sense that God would have revealed this in some form from the beginning. Both the Bridegroom and the bride entered salvation history in concrete ways two millennia ago—Christ, at the Annunciation, and the Church, from His pierced side on the cross—but both have antecedents that precede the Incarnation. We see with spiritual hindsight indications of the bride and Bridegroom throughout the history of the faithful people of Israel.

As the Nicene Creed states, the Son is "eternally begotten of the Father, God from God, true God from true God," and "through Him all things were made." There never was a time when the Son did not exist. He was God before the foundations of the world were laid, perfectly happy in communion with His Father and the Holy Spirit.

The "fullness of time" indicated when, according to God's plan, Providence would make manifest the means necessary to our salvation. In a particular corner of the world, at the ordained time, God entrusted His Son to the Virgin Mary—she who was a fitting vessel for the God-man. Her "yes" changed the world, despite her obscurity, and her faith in the promise of God laid the foundation for the faith of the entire Church that would follow. What she treasured in reverent silence God made manifest, and His plan unfolded according to the Scriptures that she knew so well.

As for the Church, both her creation and her perfection stem from God, and it is important to acknowledge her mystical and transcendent link to God's plan and Christ's salvific mission. The bride of Christ has a soul: "the 'soul' of the Church is the Holy Spirit."[1] Unlike the soul of each person, which is created by God at his or her conception, the soul of the Church is the Third Person of the Blessed Trinity—uncreated, without a beginning. Thus we can surmise that the Church was awaiting an incarnation in a similar way that the Son was—in the fullness of time—and in some mysterious way was present from the dawn of time.

Since the Church was to be born from the side of Christ after His Passion, she would have been foreshadowed in the Old Testament similar to the way that He was. We find images of Christ in the suffering servant (see Isaiah 53), the paschal lamb (Exodus 12:1–13), the spurned husband (Hosea 6:4), the Good Shepherd (Psalm 23) and elsewhere. Likewise, his bride is found throughout Scriptures in various forms, such as Zion (Psalm 50:2; Isaiah 1:8), a weeping mother (Jeremiah 31:15–17), the city of Jerusalem (Psalm 122) and the unfaithful wife (Hosea 1:2–3). Each reference has its context and lesson, which we must study in order to augment our understanding of the feminine vocation.

As we ponder these images, we must have some ideas as a backdrop so that we see the many layers of the feminine paradigm: the Church as infallible bride; the Virgin Mary, who was without sin; Eve, who was the first bride and fell from grace; the particular churches who strive to serve Christ but suffer the effects of sin; Jerusalem given as mother and refuge of the chosen people of Israel (most profoundly manifested in the temple); the Church as a foreshadowing of heaven itself; and each particular woman who is given the choice to serve her Creator as image of the bride. In this way the reader can grasp the ideal and yet accept the limits placed on us due to original sin.

BELOVED JERUSALEM

To begin, we can take a portion of Scripture that is rich in bridal imagery, taken from the book of Tobit:

> Let all men speak,
>> and give him thanks in Jerusalem.
> O Jerusalem, the holy city,
>> he will afflict you for the deeds of your sons,
>> but again he will show mercy to the sons of the righteous.
> Give thanks worthily to the Lord, and praise the King of the ages,
>> that his tent may be raised for you again with joy.
> May he cheer those within you who are captives,
>> and love those within you who are distressed,
>> to all generations for ever.
> Many nations will come from afar to the name of the Lord God,
>> bearing gifts in their hands, gifts for the King of heaven.
> Generations of generations will give you joyful praise....
> Rejoice and be glad for the sons of the righteous;
>> for they will be gathered together,
>> and will praise the Lord of the righteous.
> How blessed are those who love you!
>> They will rejoice in your peace.
> Blessed are those who grieved over all your afflictions;
>> for they will rejoice for you upon seeing all your glory,
>> and they will be made glad for ever.
> Let my soul praise God the great King.
> For Jerusalem will be built with sapphires and emeralds,
>> her walls with precious stones,
>> and her towers and battlements with pure gold.
> (Tobit 13:8–11, 13–16)

Even in this short passage we see many of the layers mentioned above: spousal love, motherhood, familial relationship among all the children of the covenant, the focus on a particular setting as source of life and appropriate place to give thanks, the singularity of the chosen ones and universal praise of all generations for the faithful bride, who will receive gifts appropriate for the King's chosen one. There are also the necessary references to the wayward children, their chastisement and their ultimate return to the fold, which permeate all of salvation history, both before and after Christ.

Mary of Nazareth, who was steeped in the Scripture and traditions of the chosen people, brought forth her canticle linking her motherhood to the motherhood of Jerusalem, to the ark hidden in the temple and to the song of Zion carried in the hearts of all who loved the God of Israel: "For behold, henceforth all generations will call me blessed; for he who is mighty has done great things for me, and holy is his name" (Luke 1:48–49). Her song of joy echoes the very passage above, which reminds us, "How blessed are those who love you, /...for they will rejoice for you upon seeing all your glory, / and they will be made glad for ever."

Jerusalem—the heart of the Israelite community chosen for special favor by God—had implications beyond the immediate community. Just as the Jews were entrusted with the covenant, which prepared the world for the Bridegroom and Savior, Jerusalem was the antecedent of the Church and heart of the bride, wherein all who chose to follow the Lamb would gather. In the words of the *Catechism*, "The people descended from Abraham would be the trustees of the promise made to the patriarchs, the chosen people, called to prepare for that day when God would gather all his children into the unity of the Church [cf. *Rom* 11:28; *Jn* 11:52; 10:16]. They would be the root onto which the Gentiles would be grafted, once they came to believe [cf. *Rom* 11:17-18, 24]" (CCC, 60).

Although the city of Jerusalem was trampled and the temple later destroyed, her spiritual destiny would not end but would undergo a transformation made possible by the blood-sacrifice of her Spouse. There her glory would shine forth before all nations in the end. The book of Revelation emphasizes this: "I saw the holy city, new Jerusalem, coming down out of heaven from God, prepared as a bride adorned for her husband" (21:2).

THE BRIDE WHO SUFFERS

A line in the passage from Tobit warrants special consideration: "O Jerusalem, the holy city, / he will afflict you for the deeds of your sons, / but again he will show mercy to the sons of the righteous" (Tobit 13:9).

There is an important incident near the end of Jesus' life recounted in the Gospel of John. He has gone up to Jerusalem for Passover, as was His custom, and He encounters the money-changers at their counters in the temple, with their animals to sell to the Jewish pilgrims for their ritual sacrifices. "And making a whip of cords, he drove them all, with the sheep and oxen, out of the temple; and he poured out the coins of the money-changers and overturned their tables. And he told those who sold the pigeons, 'Take these things away; you shall not make my Father's house a house of trade'" (John 2:15–16).

While Christ was otherwise the model of meekness and was led silent as a lamb to His slaughter, here is an example of His violent anger. He had for his entire life encountered many who lived in outright sin. He had argued with those who were obtuse concerning the Law, and even His own disciples had led him to exasperation. But this is the only time He showed such vehemence, and thus it demands an explanation.

Christ had been brought to the temple since childhood, first presented there as an infant and years later found there by his parents, conversing with teachers and scribes. Visiting the temple was an intrinsic part of the life of the Jewish people, and buying animals for sacrifice was necessary in order to meet the demands of the Law. So what did Jesus find so objectionable about these transactions?

The covenantal relationship between God and His chosen people centered on the temple, the Law and the sacrifices offered there. As we now look at this covenant with a "nuptial eye" (so to speak), we see that Jerusalem is a spiritual mother to this people, and the temple is her most sacred part—in essence, her very womb. Wouldn't the Bridegroom be outraged that the covenant manifesting the very love of God for His people had become a form of prostitution? This would have to elicit a response from Him in the name of both spousal love and chivalry.

Whereas Christ showed tenderness toward the woman caught in adultery, dismissing her accusers and admonishing her to sin no more, this event in the temple causes even the bride to suffer. There are two scourgings in the Gospels: Christ endures His horrific lashing during the Passion, but first He scourges the bride, who has sold herself and debased the covenant within her very walls. If the husband and wife are indeed one flesh, then the two scourgings overlap and become part of the same oblation for the purification of the chosen ones.

> Then came one of the seven angels...and spoke to me, saying, "Come, I will show you the Bride, the wife of the Lamb." And in the Spirit he carried me away to a great, high mountain, and showed me the holy city Jerusalem coming down out of heaven from God, having the glory of God, its radiance like a most rare jewel, like a jasper, clear as crystal.... But nothing unclean shall enter it, nor any one who practices abomination or falsehood, but only those who are written in the Lamb's book of life. (Revelation 21:9–11, 27)

Just as we will be purified before we meet God in heaven, the bride required purification in order to be worthy of the Lamb. Sin had entered in and had sullied her robes, but with the gift of Himself, Christ washed her clean in His own blood and made her worthy of His love.

Even the motherhood of Daughter Zion would be purchased in the pain and suffering Genesis forewarned (3:16), and blood and water would flow as the price of redeeming each created soul. She shared His suffering—thus even added to His suffering—but it was necessary, and her subsequent glory shows His glory all the more.

"Destroy this temple, and in three days I will raise it up" (John 2:19), said Christ, equating the sacred temple with His body and establishing an indissoluble union between Him and His bride. She felt the first lashes; He endured them next. He thus gave meaning to her suffering and to *all* sorrow. Then He shed His blood in the new and everlasting covenant to be guarded by Holy Mother Church, who was herself now without stain or blemish.

Saint John tells us that the Lord "showed me the holy city Jerusalem coming down out of heaven from God, having the glory of God" (Revelation 21:10–11). Contemporary events show that Jerusalem is still undoubtedly a city set apart and still an object of great hope, sorrow and meaning. Is it possible that this place is undergoing a scourging that has a relationship to the rejection of her Beloved?

The bride must be purified of all sin in order for her consummation with the Bridegroom to come to its ultimate fruition. Thus while all suffering has meaning, that of Jerusalem must elicit special prayer and consideration. Jerusalem is a model for all women, is related in a special way to the Church and will reveal the glory of God at the ordained time.

WISDOM IN THE OLD TESTAMENT

Wisdom, an attribute of God, is also personified as a bride throughout the Old Testament. Her created essence permeates the heavens and the earth, and yet stands apart as pure and distinct.[2]

> For she is a breath of the power of God,
> and a pure emanation of the glory of the Almighty;
> therefore nothing defiled gains entrance into her.
> For she is a reflection of eternal light,
> a spotless mirror of the working of God,
> and an image of his goodness. (Wisdom 7:25–26)

The precedence of wisdom in God's plan is made clear in Proverbs, where the author explains that creating her was "the first of his acts of old" (Proverbs 8:22):

> Before the mountains had been shaped,
>   before the hills, I was brought forth;
> before he had made the earth with its fields,
>   or the first of the dust of the world.
> When he established the heavens, I was there,
>   when he drew a circle on the face of the deep,
> when he made firm the skies above,
>   when he established the fountains of the deep,
>   when he assigned to the sea its limit,
>   so that the waters might not transgress his command,
> when he marked out the foundations of the earth,
>   then I was beside him, like a master workman;
> and I was daily his delight,
>   rejoicing before him always. (Proverbs 8:25–30)

If wisdom is the bride, which the Scriptures make patently clear, then from this portion of God's word we can see that she was God's helpmate in the rest of creation after she was brought forth. This establishes the fact that authentic femininity is an honor and a dignity far beyond our imagination. While we know that the "pearl of great price" is worthy of every sacrifice, the richness of authentic femininity is our very own jewel, our own treasure that we cannot begin to value enough.

Solomon, who wrote ecstatic refrains to the beauty of wisdom, recognized that she was the mother of all that is good (see Wisdom 7:11–12). In keeping with the laws concerning spousal love—just as the love of God and human love bear fruit—such intense love of wisdom must extend itself and breathe its inherent goodness upon creation. Wisdom, like femininity, shines like a beacon, drawing all peoples to her innate beauty.

> Wisdom has built her house,
>   she has set up her seven pillars.
> She has slaughtered her beasts, she has mixed her wine,
>   she has also set her table.
> She has sent out her maids to call
>   from the highest places in the town,
> "Whoever is simple, let him turn in here!"
>   To him who is without sense she says,
> "Come, eat of my bread
>   and drink of the wine I have mixed!
> Leave simpleness, and live,
>   and walk in the way of insight." (Proverbs 9:1–6)

This is the antecedent of the Church and of the generous hospitality and maternal love to which all women are called in their diverse paths through life. Once the guests come to her abode, they will find life and peace. Just as Holy Mother Church spreads a banquet provided by the Bridegroom, Lady Wisdom offers a counsel not of her own making but one whose ultimate source is God Himself. She distributes morsels from His storehouses and comforts souls with His grace. Her caresses are tangible reflections of His life-giving love for her, which cannot help but spill over into all of creation. What bride, knowing her place in creation and the esteem of God for her, would not be both humble and joyful in her vocation!

Wisdom is the foundation of the Law and the Prophets and their crowning glory. God's plan for his people was revealed in detail for their own good, so that they would thrive among the nations and the relationship between the two parties in the covenant would prosper. Sometimes the community would adhere to the commandments of God more closely than at other times, and sometimes one would be hard-pressed to distinguish the Jewish remnant from its neighbors. But in time the people would return to their faith, and they would cling once more to the special covenant with the one true God who called them out of darkness.

To help the people see what lay shrouded in the Scriptures, the spiritual covenant even took tangible form, especially in the yearly celebration called "Rejoicing in the Torah." During this feast, in Hebrew called *Simchat Torah*, "one takes the Torah under one's arm, as if it were a bride, and dances with it in the synagogue."[3] The men who participate are actually called "bridegrooms of the Torah," which underscores the nuptial reality. The day allows the community to celebrate God's mercy anew and to acknowledge that it is Lady Wisdom who gave life to the children of Israel.[4]

For all the passionate love bound up in this earthy and joyful feast, the care taken with the actual Torah throughout the centuries reveals that there is a chasteness to this love, an abiding reverence for the Law as bride. The scrolls are treated with great respect. They are kept in an ark-like tabernacle—often, fittingly, with a crown adorning it. The Law forbids anyone from touching them.

When the scrolls are removed each day so that a portion of the Law may be read to the assembly, they are never laid on a bare table but always on a prepared cloth. Then there are layers to be reverently removed: first a mantle, often finely embroidered, then an outer covering of expensive material and then a girdle of silk, which ties the scrolls together. At this point a silver bar is used as a marker, recalling the admonition of God that nothing should ever touch the ark, which rested in the midst of the chosen people.[5] The Jewish men, who love wisdom with the ardor of a husband, go so far as to lay down their lives to protect their scrolls, as witnessed by tragedies over the centuries in which many sons of Israel died in trying to rescue them from fire or abuse.

Jesus, upon reaching the age of maturity, read from the Torah and even unlocked its mysteries in a way that astonished those assembled. He knew the Scriptures intimately, of course, since He was the Author, Creator and Spouse of the wisdom therein. He would later stress to his followers that he did not intend to do away with even the smallest portion of the Law, saying, "For truly, I say to you, till heaven and earth pass away, not an iota, not a dot, will pass from the law until all is accomplished" (Matthew 5:18).

Indeed, if Jesus had allowed such a thing to happen, He would have distorted or erased the very features of His own bride. Rather He reminded us that all of the Law and the Prophets could be summarized in the love of God and of neighbor. Understanding this allows us to more easily grasp the truth that the revealed laws of God were simply tangible dimensions of the bride of the ages, whom He could embrace as easily as a rabbi did his beloved scrolls.

WOMEN OF THE OLD TESTAMENT

While Judaism is without a doubt a patriarchal religion, it would not have fulfilled the plan of God without countless faithful women who exemplified wisdom, courage and strength. Interestingly, Jewish law prescribed strict rules about the mixing of the sexes, dietary laws, marriage requirements and family life, and most of the Jewish women highlighted in the Scriptures were unconventional in the sense that they respected the Law and the reason for its existence but used it cleverly to circumvent difficult situations. They managed to preserve both the Law and their families using their wisdom and wits. The honor shown these women is almost a wry appreciation of the fact that the Law was made for man and not man for the Law, while cherishing the love of God, which formed the backdrop to circumstances.

Sarah, the wife of Abraham, has long been credited with being a teacher of the faith to other Jewish women. When the time came for her own "visitation," God made her the mother of the promise, despite her advanced age. She treated her three visitors to generous hospitality. Their conversation with Abraham over the child to be conceived (which she overheard and participated in through the tent flap) shares similarities with the angel Gabriel's visit to the Blessed Mother. Sarah's personality shines through, even thousands of years later, and God rewarded her patience beyond all expectations (see Genesis 18:1–15).

Rebekah, Rachel and Leah participated in the building of the covenant, though not without strife and suffering. They were, for their own part, hospitable to life and strong in personality, and they tried to thwart the forces that threatened the stability of their families. God wove His will in and out of the strength and foibles of His particular chosen ones, showing His own patience and ability to "work all things together unto good" (see Genesis chapters 24 and 29).

Moses, who is credited with leading the children of Israel out of slavery, would not have survived without the critical assistance of at least six women. He encountered danger through no fault of his own but due to circumstances allowed by God—circumstances that proved the wisdom and courage of those around him, who would not sacrifice life despite frightening pressure.

Early in his life two midwives disobeyed a direct order to kill the boy children (see Exodus 1:15–20). Then his mother and sister hid him in the river, and the daughter of Pharoah found him there and took him as her own (Exodus 2:2–10). Later Moses' wife, Zipporah, saved him by circumcising their son (Exodus 4:24–26).

Many women who faced barrenness begged God to be entrusted with life: Sarah, Rebekah, Rachel, Leah, Samson's unnamed mother and Hannah (see Judges 13:2–25; 1 Samuel 1:1—2:10). Their faithful pleading was ultimately rewarded with the birth of sons who were all key participants in the covenant between God and His chosen people. Rather than turning their backs on physical motherhood, which didn't seem to be a gift that God was offering them, they believed firmly that it was essential to their holiness and a critical way to do their share for the survival of Israel. After years, even decades of fervent prayer, they were each rewarded with life.

A HEROIC MOTHER

Finally we come to the example of the mother of the seven sons in the Second Book of Maccabees. This is an account rich with meaning and layered with references to the beauty and strength of authentic femininity.

As a backdrop one must understand that the Jewish people and their temple were under a siege that had lasted for decades. One by one the Maccabeus brothers—first Judas, then Jonathan, then Simon—took up the sword to defend what was dearest to them. "They come against us in great pride and lawlessness to destroy us and our wives and our children, and to despoil us; but we fight for our lives and our laws" (1 Maccabees 3:20–21). These laws were the embodiment of wisdom, as previously shown, and "it is no light thing to show irreverence to the divine laws—a fact which later events will make clear" (2 Maccabees 4:17).

In fact, there was a twofold attack on the chosen people: the efforts to separate them from their laws and, the crowning blow, to deface the sanctuary of the temple. When this happened on various occasions, there was no limit to their grief. At one point in the struggle, "they saw the sanctuary desolate, the altar profaned, and the gates burned. In the courts they saw bushes sprung up as in a thicket, or as on one of the mountains. They saw also the chambers of the priests in ruins. Then they rent their clothes, and mourned with great lamentation, and sprinkled themselves with ashes" (1 Maccabees 4:38–39).

The effrontery—virtually spiritual rape—was beyond what faithful Jews could bear, since the temple was sanctuary, their mother, the resting place of the ark and the very font of their spiritual life.

> Harsh and utterly grievous was the onslaught of evil. For the temple was filled with debauchery and reveling by the Gentiles, who dallied with harlots and had intercourse with women within the sacred precincts, and besides brought in things for sacrifice that were unfit. The altar was covered with abominable offerings which were forbidden by the laws. A man could neither keep the sabbath, nor observe the feasts of his fathers, nor so much as confess himself to be a Jew. (2 Maccabees 6:3–6)

By the thousands the men of Israel went to the defense of the bride, and by the thousands they fell, though not without scattered victories and short respites in which they could rededicate the temple. One of these times, commemorated at Hannukah, Judas Maccabeus regained Jerusalem for his people and set about the work of restoring dignity and honor to the sanctuary. First they rid the temple of all foreign objects and built a brand-new interior, complete with sanctuary and altar, gates and decorations. There was great rejoicing over the rededication, complete with music and feasting (see 1 Maccabees 4:42–61).[6]

The cleansing of the temple was not to last. More battles raged, and Jerusalem was overrun. It was during a very low point that a heroic family, consisting of a mother and her seven sons, was captured and pressured to break the Jewish dietary laws. One by one the young men were tortured and killed in front of their mother, yet neither she nor they would yield, proclaiming that they were "ready to die rather than transgress the laws of our fathers" (2 Maccabees 7:2).

When the last son was brought before the mother, the persecutors implored her to convince him to save himself. Her resolve, however, was firm:

> My son, have pity on me. I carried you nine months in my womb, and nursed you for three years, and have reared you and brought you up to this point in your life, and have taken care of you. I beseech you, my child, to look at the heaven and the earth and see everything that is in them, and recognize that God did not make them out of things that existed. Thus also mankind comes into being. Do not fear this butcher, but prove worthy of your brothers. Accept death, so that in God's mercy I may get you back again with your brothers. (2 Maccabees 7:27–29)

What more perfect embodiment of femininity could be found? This mother had offered material and spiritual sustenance to her loved ones, was a font of courage and wisdom and exercised unwavering faith in the promises of God. Nothing could deter her from doing the right thing under the circumstances, and she compelled her sons to do likewise. Unlike the other examples of Jewish women, she didn't resort to cleverness but stood solidly for goodness and life on God's terms.

THE OLD TESTAMENT AND CONTEMPORARY WOMEN

It is abundantly clear that the bridal imagery found in Holy Mother Church is older than creation itself and is as far-flung as the Spirit of God, which cannot be contained. Just as the Church fathers recognized that there are shards of truth to be found in myriad places, even by those who have never heard of the gospel of Christ, the Old Testament writers knew that wisdom knew no parochial bounds. Inexhaustible yet accessible, her home is in Jerusalem, but her waters flow abundantly in all directions.

Sirach explains this by linking her life-giving waters to the known rivers, among them the Euphrates, the Nile, the Jordan and the Tigris. These flow into the sea, an abyss deep enough to satisfy all those who love truth and cherish life (see Sirach 24:23–29). Thousands of years later the book of Revelation built upon this concept: "Then he showed me the river of the water of life, bright as crystal, flowing from the throne of God and of the Lamb through the middle of the street of the city; also, on either side of the river, the tree of life" (Revelation 22:1–2). This imagery binds Lady Wisdom, our first mother, Eve, Mary, the new "mother of the living," and the temple into the spousal embrace.

So what does this mean for each woman—today, tomorrow, always? Clearly there is a great honor offered in establishing a feminine image as the seat of wisdom. It would be incumbent on each of us to immerse ourselves in wisdom: the wisdom of Scripture, the wisdom of Tradition, the wisdom of relationships, the wisdom of suffering. The beauty of femininity is our ability to relate the truths of God to others because of the trust that souls place in us—from children to coworkers to friends, even to strangers.

The well of knowledge from which we draw in conversations and how we comport ourselves from day to day will transmit either the truths of God or something darker. Even the Old Testament speaks of the female figure of "folly," who also extends an invitation. "But her food is not truth and discipline. She offers deceit and wanton pleasure. The consequence of eating at her table is not life but death."[7] We have to choose what we want to offer to those we meet, and those who trust us for nourishment will benefit by our wisdom or suffer for our folly.

Redemption is part of God's message for women. Time and again the temple in Jerusalem was profaned, and yet each time it was rededicated. Modern women must take this message to heart, for the errors we make—especially in the realm of our own purity—we can rectify with contrition and sacramental confession. The Israelites strayed from observance of the law and yet returned to God, who embraced them each time without hesitation. The same is true for us when we wander from the true path. We can grow through our mistakes and learn from the suffering that poor choices bring to us and our loved ones. "[I]n everything God works for good with those who love him" (Romans 8:28).

Jesus looks upon each of us as radiant brides, entrusting us with the task of representing the highest good: wisdom itself. In the eschatological scheme He embraces wisdom as He would his own cherished love. We can embody this wisdom or refuse the honor.

God offers the examples of women such as Deborah, Judith and Mary as the highest ideals of courageous obedience and life-giving faith. Self-indulgence and wanton disobedience look shallow compared to the real fulfillment that wisdom provides. Reflecting His glory through the pursuit of wisdom both serves Him and lifts us to a dignity we hardly deserve. This is the backbone and treasure of femininity.

CHAPTER EIGHT

The Church as Builder of Culture

An important dimension of the Church that has been recognized throughout her history is her ability to bear culture to the world. Even under persecution and amid trials and great suffering, the faithful have been responsible for order, for transcribing familial relationships into stable landmarks and for creating beauty, both at the service of the liturgy and for the edification of the world at large. To women who wish to live out their vocations most fully and thereby image the Church in all her dimensions, it is obvious that "creating culture" is work that we are fully capable of doing—and doing very well.

Philosopher Joseph Pieper reminds us that the foundations of culture are based on how we perceive God, which leads us to a particular *cultus*, or ritual.[1] Christian culture must take the theological and philosophical truths that we believe and enflesh them, so that the immortal and invisible God is incarnate in daily life. What we celebrate, how we worship and the choices we make are all key to the culture that will emerge—for better or worse.

THE ENDURING STRENGTH OF CULTURE

According to George Weigel, biographer of John Paul II, one critical change that came with Karol Wojtyla's election to the papacy was the fresh premise he brought to the understanding of the identity of the Church. Until then most believed that world history was driven by economic and military power. This pope's firsthand experience of the Polish nation—which continued to exist despite the years of its complete eradication from the map—made him recognize that culture itself was more important than any form of secular power.[2]

During the twenty-six years of his papacy, John Paul II revolutionized the way that the Church interacted with the world, relying on her cultural influence to transmit the truths of the faith in myriad venues that hadn't been emphasized before. His personal experience proved invaluable in navigating the landscape of post-war political relations, since he had seen that the "cultural resistance" of the Polish people in recent centuries had proved far harder for their enemies to calculate and defend against than any other opposition—even diplomatic showdowns or military confrontations.

Much of this resistance was founded on the Polish people's dedication to their literary giants, such as Adam Mickiewicz (1798–1855), an exiled playwright, and Henry Sienkiewicz (1846–1916), who wrote among other things *Quo Vadis* and a historical trilogy that brought to life the Polish heroes of the seventeenth century. Both of these writers' prolific works were banned in subsequent times of oppression, yet both were pivotal in the education of Karol Wojtyla and his contemporaries. They endured both Nazi and Communist persecution by keeping alive and building upon the cultural ideals of Poland's past.

This intersects with the feminine vocation precisely because of the great contribution that women make to the building of culture. John Paul II's affection for women and the confidence he placed in them was made clear in *Evangelium Vitae*: "In transforming culture so that it supports life, women occupy a place, in thought and action, which is unique and decisive."[3] He went on to define further the critical task for women:

> Women first learn and then teach others that human relations are authentic if they are open to accepting the other person: a person who is recognized and loved because of the dignity which comes from being a person and not from other considerations, such as usefulness, strength, intelligence, beauty or health. This is the fundamental contribution which the Church and humanity expect from women. And it is the indispensable prerequisite for an authentic cultural change.[4]

We must acknowledge the trust the Church places in us and then use our feminine genius to discern how best, practically, to build this culture, which the world so desperately needs for its spiritual and physical health. We must refuse to be daunted by the task ahead and concentrate on our own families and immediate communities, for what could be euphemistically seen as rebuilding the culture "brick by brick" is essentially "soul by soul."

Mother Teresa could have been overwhelmed by the needs of her first outpost of charity. But she simply focused on picking up the first body and only after that the second—and so forth. With God's grace and His gift of fortitude, she reached dozens, scores and ultimately countless thousands.

FAITH CANNOT ENDURE WITHOUT CULTURE

Author Robert Louis Wilken looked at the history of the early Church and the way that Christians built culture around their faith in order to nourish it. He goes so far as to say that faith cannot be sustained without a supportive culture, which makes sense given the difficulties contemporary Christians face in an increasingly hostile environment.

Wilken defines culture as "the pattern of inherited meanings and sensibilities encoded in rituals, law, language, practices, and stories that can order, inspire, and guide the behavior, thoughts, affectations of a Christian people."[5] He stresses that culture has various dimensions, but he shows how Holy Mother Church in her earliest years breathed sanctifying grace into *place*, *time* and *language*, each one essential to the sacramental vision.[6]

Wilken gives concrete historical illustrations for this thesis: for example, the creation of *sacred spaces*, beginning with the catacomb of Saint Callistus in the early third century; the adoption of the *Christian calendar* in the seventh century; and the constant effort by monastics to preserve and spread their *rich body of knowledge*, which could have been lost in the dissolution of the Roman Empire.

These examples form an excellent starting point as we look at our lives and the influence we can bring to bear in our own circumstances. God calls us to reflect his truths written in the universe by sanctifying place, time and language: "The heavens are telling the glory of God; / and the firmament proclaims his handiwork. / Day to day pours forth speech, / and night to night declares knowledge" (Psalm 19:1–2).

SACRED SPACE IN THE DOMESTIC CHURCH

To consider the first example of building culture—the appropriation of space in which to give glory and honor to God—there is much that every woman can do to affect the atmosphere of her surroundings. Each Catholic dwelling, whether it be a house, an apartment or a bare room, should reflect the order inherent in God's creation. This order gives dignity to the space's inhabitants.

An underlying simplicity in these settings helps focus the hearts of family and visitors alike on the straightforwardness of the gospel, which is ordered to love of God and love of neighbor. Well-chosen religious articles serve to lift hearts and minds to God, the Source of our very being. Without redundancy or excess, an image of Christ or a crucifix, a picture of a saint or even a stitched prayer can remind those who pass through that there is more to this world than what is apparent to the senses.

Considering that tastes vary and one should be drawn in a personal way through art and imagery, children should be encouraged when old enough to choose their own pictures or icons so that they have a special connection to God's holy realm. A mother should discuss the child's particular choice of an image before adding it to the room. And if the child offers the item to a priest for a blessing, it will always hold a special meaning. Mothers then can teach about the decorum and acts of piety that accompany such things, allowing the objects to actually become channels of grace for those who are properly disposed. This will create a quiet but lasting impact on young souls especially, and God will use this leaven for His own end.

There is an abundance of information available to those who want to enhance their living spaces. Television executives, magazine editors and book publishers have invested heavily in this niche, making it easier than ever to make our surroundings beautiful and highly functional. Women should take advantage of the abundant material on redecorating, decluttering, improving and streamlining our living spaces, both inside and out. As a backdrop to our projects, we can remember that, more than simply applying paint or tidying closets, we "baptize" these endeavors, building sacred spaces for the domestic church and thereby building a culture that makes room for authentic love.

One woman with a number of small children recognized that the disorder in family scheduling, constant tardiness and rebellion over chores was not due to malice or deliberate vice but to having too many possessions. Her children wanted to obey her directive to "clean your room," but it was simply impossible. One day the mother stepped in to "help" her daughter clean her room, and even she was overwhelmed. Not only did the toys not have adequate space for storage, but the clothes didn't fit in the drawers. And with Christmas looming, she realized that it was only going to get worse.

Thankfully, with spiritual direction, the mother realized that she was guilty of hoarding—belying trust in God and teaching her children to look to material goods for consolation. After taking several vanloads of toys and clothing to a local thrift shop, everyone in the family could order their lives and manage schedules in a timely fashion, while learning both to trust in God and to value simplicity.

Of course, we must be conscious of the temptation to spend too much time or money to create the unreal perfection that is occasionally promoted in the media. The atmosphere we create is simply a means to an end. Rather than becoming slaves to our possessions, we must allow the items God has entrusted to our care to serve us in our efforts to become saints.

MARKING THE HOURS IN A CHRISTIAN HOME

The second realm that women can baptize is that of time. The early Church began by setting aside the Lord's Day to mark the Resurrection, which was initially so fresh in their minds. Their devotion to the importance of Sunday set them apart from a world that either followed pagan rituals or honored the Jewish Sabbath.

When Our Lady appeared to shepherd children in La Salette, France, in 1846, she wept over the fact that the faithful had abandoned the third commandment—keeping the Lord's Day holy—to their own peril. We cannot count on legislation to restrict activities on Sundays that interfere with the worship of God, so it is incumbent on each of us to set limits for ourselves.

Beyond honoring the Sabbath, in the earliest centuries the Church also marked time, organizing hours into the Divine Office and entire seasons into the liturgical year. Likewise we can order the day with prayers that are appropriate for our family members, for as Edith Stein noted, "the life of an authentic Catholic woman is also a liturgical life."[7] Mothers have a particular sensibility for this, knowing how children cling to ritual and are comforted by it. We can begin our family's day with a short morning offering, give a few minutes at noon to Our Lady through the Angelus and begin each meal with some words of thanks to the Giver of all good things. Evening prayer, joining hearts in specific intentions, will prepare little ones for a peaceful bedtime.

Days that have this eternal backdrop will comfort souls in ways that we cannot gauge. Such is the foundation of building culture, since all time is a gift of God and should be sanctified in its passing.

Sacred time is also recalled in the various devotions we adopt to celebrate various feasts, participate in suggested fasts and mark the seasons of the Church year, so that all can live in their own way the life of Christ. Women, the keepers of the family calendars, can appropriate this task on a personal level by marking name days, baptismal days and anniversaries of special spiritual events. In the same way that holy spaces will reflect the unique charisms of each family, celebrations will breathe forth their God-given personality.

One fascinating detail concerning those who have rejected Christianity as a creed shouldn't be surprising. These individuals may not want Christ and the demands of discipleship, but they realize that they and their offspring are suffering from a dearth of rituals. For example, those who have no intention of baptizing their children now find themselves with one less party, one less celebration to share with friends and family. In Europe this has given rise to "naming celebrations," an invented ritual to welcome children into the community with equal pomp (and presents) but without ties to an "oppressive" religion. Interestingly, names of babies—which were once ties to patron saints or family members—are equally disengaged from Christian culture. In fact, they often hearken back to pre-Christian themes, real or imagined.

It is obvious that the thirst for ritual endures. The heart longs to mark time and events in the company of loved ones. Whatever culture blossoms will be an organic reflection of our beliefs, so it is essential that we order the events in our lives to reflect authentic revelation.

We should look to the Church for guidance—the Church that has been building culture for two millennia—so that our rituals will breathe the triune God. The more we study the truths of our faith, the more we can find ways to integrate them into our celebrations large and small. Our family traditions and seemingly humble rituals will root our culture in rich soil and bring about lasting fruit for the harvest.

COMMUNICATING THE TRUTHS OF THE CHURCH

In the last chapter, on woman as image of the Church as teacher, I stressed the importance of language as a part of overall education. The Church has a unique vocabulary, which women initially are responsible for teaching to their children in conjunction with how the ideas therein relate to the secular world. There are countless words that are unique to transmitting the truths of our faith, there are concepts that broaden the individual and there are virtues that, when offered for emulation, challenge people to heights that are otherwise unknown.

I have heard from language experts that approximately 90 percent of our conversation uses the same one hundred words. What a sad thought, considering the richness of the human language. It is also discouraging to know that the most basic of Bible stories are increasingly unknown among the younger generation. Further, we see already that the twentieth century is becoming ancient history to many. If even this most recent storehouse of information is already unappreciated, what of the previous nineteen centuries and the invaluable lessons that they have provided in the expansion and deepening of Christian thought?

Establishing a comprehensive vocabulary in the home is an excellent start in building and preserving culture, for where words lead, ideas follow. Reading good stories; creating a historical framework as a learning backdrop; sharing the treasures of the Bible and pointing out references to them wherever they are found; exposing young minds to the vast array of virtues, the distinctions among them and how and when they can be used; visiting historical landmarks and museums; and talking with friends and family—especially the elderly—about their memories can inspire little ones to reach beyond popular culture for truths that nourish the heart. Even the concepts of manliness in young boys, femininity in little girls and courage in doing what goes against the grain in everyday life can launch youngsters to strive for the deep satisfaction that comes from finding God's will for their lives.

Women, especially mothers, provide a bridge between their children and the world. Edith Stein recognized that language was an intrinsic part of the process.[8] All women share the mission to the family: aunts, grandmothers, godmothers and then trusted teachers and friends. Women should recognize the remarkable task God entrusts to us, the privilege of sifting all that has been handed to us over the centuries and offering the very best of it to the next generation. We cannot take this responsibility lightly.

Introductions, meals, social engagements, academic interactions and business transactions can be opportunities to establish rituals, which at their heart declare that the "other" is worthy of respect. This begins in the home, starting with using *please* and *thank you*. It evolves into proper playground behavior, kindness, respect for authority and the property of others, as well as learning to be comfortable in a variety of situations.

The ultimate goal of etiquette is to enhance the dignity of the person. Etiquette can be a tremendous vehicle for ordering the culture along the proper lines. It certainly has the capacity for being abused or misunderstood when it becomes reduced to "manners" or "protocol," or when it becomes detached from charity. Scorning those who don't know the proper use of silverware, frowning on those whose choice of dress indicates a misunderstanding of events or feeling superior to those who have not had access to particular social institutions is using etiquette as a cudgel rather than a form of healthy interaction. Many use the rituals of etiquette as a handy way to divide the initiated from the uninitiated, making others feel alienated rather than embraced.

One college-aged daughter delighted in bringing a young man to church with her family, knowing that he had fallen away from the practice of his faith. Her little victory was crushed by her mother, who couldn't get past the fact that he was inappropriately dressed on his foray back to the sacraments. True enough, one's choice of clothing signals his understanding of the object of worship, but at the outset the daughter recognized a hierarchy of goods, beginning with bringing this young man into the presence of God. Sadly, the imagined opprobrium of her contemporaries was more important to the mother that day, and the young man sensed it. He did not return to that church again.

As long as manners are taught in a way that serves the person, they can be intuited practically. Teaching etiquette should be combined with reminding children to read the details of different circumstances, details that are often very subtle. While never compromising in showing our respect for God or the things of God, we must learn to adapt to our surroundings so that others feel accepted and loved.

CULTURE AND CLOTHING

The domestic church does embrace the world eventually, and here is where the culture nourished within is put on display, revealing deep truths about the dignity of the human person. Beauty and elegance span an array of styles and tastes, but there are some common elements that should guide us in our efforts to enhance our own attractiveness so as to draw others to a better understanding of what our faith teaches us.

The everyday dress of women should work to their advantage and call to mind the inherent dignity of a child of God. There is tremendous latitude in style today, but few current fashions really flatter women. From nearly indecent clothing once restricted to red-light districts to androgynous athletic gear, young women are pushed into choosing styles that make social statements that may be far from what they have in mind.

A group of college students were drawn to a weekend retreat outside of Boston that was advertised as entering into "The World of Jane Austen." Shyly they arrived in their bulky sweats, curious and open but unsure of how they would acclimate to a few days in the early nineteenth century. Costumes were there for the choosing, and slowly the students adapted to defined waistlines, lace, yards of draped fabric—and bonnets! They greeted these items at first with reticence and giggles, but a few hours in the costumes brought out a surprised reaction: femininity and graceful living can be liberating.

Upon reflection, the students realized that contemporary fashions had boxed them into two options: sexual flirtatiousness or ungainly layers. Knowing the former was morally unacceptable, they had retreated into the latter. Reaching into another era opened their eyes about their own femininity and the need to forge a middle path emphasizing dignity and self-respect.

It would serve us and our daughters well to reject the styles that denigrate or sexualize us. This might require some research and learning to sew, but it is possible to follow general styles while avoiding excesses. The point is not to stigmatize anyone or set her apart as priggish but to take full advantage of the individuality that mass media encourage, to break from contemporary trends and pursue what is both flattering and modest.

Of course, adolescents, for whom this is most important, are loathe to depart from the "groupthink" that dominates their world. For them a key part of the message may be that the life of virtue requires making difficult decisions and finding the strength to be a people set apart.

A gratifying dimension of these efforts would undoubtedly be a surprised and positive response from men, who have been forced to fight their hard-wired responses to women's flirty playfulness at every turn. Indeed, in order for women to be taken seriously—beginning with eye contact—we would do well to cover the overexposed skin that is so distracting to others. If we want to be seen as more than a collection of body parts, perhaps we could drape them appropriately and engage men in a higher form of interaction. The initiative must be ours, and the response would satisfy everyone.

A CULTURE FOUNDED ON PRAYER

Even from the outset the Church was feminine, and recognized her mission: "In the catacombs the Church is often represented as a woman in prayer, arms outstretched in the praying position. Like Christ who stretched out his arms on the cross, through him, with him, and in him, she offers herself and intercedes for all men" (CCC, 1368).

Whatever effort we expend in building culture, it must be grounded in prayer and lifted to God as a gift from our hearts. Just as it is essential that a mother nourish herself adequately so that she can nurse her infant, a woman has to dedicate herself to her own prayer life, constantly deepening her union with God, because only then can she feed and direct the souls in her spiritual care.[9] There can be no room for pride in our projects; rather we must humbly cling to faith alone, which will guide properly the work of our hands.

Henri de Lubac speaks eloquently of the faith of the Bride, which "was Christ's gift to her, to be a power glowing inside her, at once her origin and her sustaining—a faith we profess individually only by associating ourselves with the whole Church."[10] This faith is expressed by the Church in the manner of a faithful wife who is parted from her spouse and "who bears witness to him, prays to him, longs for sight of him, and waits for his second coming."[11] Moreover, Holy Mother Church is with child, often suffering as expectant mothers do, spiritually united to the Bridegroom who planted the seed and anxious to share joy with Him over a safe delivery.

The rich theology of our Catholic faith teaches us that our works and our sufferings both become prayer when offered to Christ, and they will bear fruit when united to His own redemptive work. Thus most prayer is unspoken; it is simply lived. Conversation with God can be constant and, tied to the mundane, to everyday life, lifted to the realm of the infinite with a union of hearts at its center.

Women in all states of life can readily understand this longing founded in hope and love. We petition on behalf of ourselves, our family members, our friends and coworkers, the homeless man seen briefly through the car window, the tragic faces seen on the evening news. We must want what is best for all of God's children, although sometimes He alone knows what that is. We carry these petitions in our hearts and lay them at the foot of the altar at every opportunity, knowing that our compassionate God will listen and respond.

THE CULTURE OF JOYFUL ANTICIPATION

Mary's time of waiting during the first Advent is instructive for the whole Church. During the months between the Annunciation and the birth of Our Lord, she lived in quiet but joyful expectation, pondering the intimate contact with God Himself, her understanding of His promises and the realities of a future life with the holy Child. While wondering about many things, each day was sufficient unto itself. Her only known action was that of service to her aging cousin, who was facing her own momentous event, the birth of her long-awaited child.

The liturgy links Mary's life leading to Christ's nativity first with the previous four thousand years of anticipation of the Messiah, and then with our own expectation of His Second Coming at the consummation of the world. Waiting is inevitable in our temporal sphere, and Mary shows us how to do it well. She takes each day with docility and faith and uses the time cheerfully and charitably.

Mary is not impatient or irritable, nor does she waste time in idle thought. God's timing cannot and should not be rushed, and Mary reminds us to think about the future with trust. "When he humbled himself to come among us as a man, he fulfilled the plan you formed long ago and opened for us the way to salvation. Now we watch for the day, hoping that the salvation promised us will be ours when Christ our Lord will come again in his glory."[12]

With the patience of the Church—which Our Lady perfectly exemplifies—we must learn to let the fruits of our labors be manifest in God's time. We teach our children, we lay the foundations of simple piety and build the culture according to our understanding of God, but we may not see the anticipated results. In a fallen world, with its abuse of human freedom, our efforts may seem wasted.

Yet how many of us took years, perhaps decades, to recognize the patient love of a mother or grandmother and her deeds of charity? Many of us, sadly, lacked appreciation until after they were long dead. Such is the nature of family life. But just as Mary walked in darkness without knowing the details of God's plan, we too walk by faith and not by sight.

We must keep in mind that the primary duty of the bride is to serve the Bridegroom, and that all we do we give as a gift in His name. There are no guarantees about the outcome, but we should trust God's word that nothing is wasted.

CULTURE: A MEANS TO AN END

In building culture we have to remember that each element is simply a means to an end. The point of dressing well, of creating beauty, of marking time, of teaching manners and of baptizing the mundane is ultimately to reflect the infinite, to point souls toward their Creator. We cannot become trapped in the details or allow the means to absorb us inordinately.

Culture will be successful as long as it establishes unity among believers, helps create harmony in the home and has charity and simplicity as its themes. It will manifest the authentic love of the Bridegroom through the maternal warmth of the bride, drawing creation into the divine embrace and showering it with truth.

As Wilken noted, "If Christian culture is to be renewed, habits are more vital than revivals, rituals more edifying than spiritual highs."[13] Habits, rituals and celebrations begin at home—around the hearth and imbued with the warmth of family love.

CHAPTER NINE

Pitfalls to Authentic Femininity

What could be more beautiful than a bride arrayed for her husband, a mother suckling her child, a religious sister teaching eager young students, a ballerina renowned for her beauty and grace on stage? If these are the gems in the crown of womanhood, who could think of rejecting the feminine vocation?

While the hearts and souls of women are essential to the health and well-being of families and society, generosity of spirit comes with a host of pitfalls, given the realities of a fallen world. Through firsthand experience we know that every gesture of help can be twisted and the very gift of self can be abused.

How many stories do we hear of ungrateful children, boorish husbands and authentic love scorned? (Women, too, certainly can harbor harsh, cruel or ungrateful attitudes.) Think of the troops of generous consecrated women pouring themselves out in vocations of service, only to die forgotten and lonely. We must be realistic: If we promote the generous gift of self as bedrock for the vocation of woman, we must be prepared to be rejected, misunderstood and even despised.

What is essential is the focus with which the woman as bride loves and imitates her Spouse, Christ the Lord. If she loves others for love of Him, she will not be disappointed. If she gives to Him as she finds Him in those in need, He will receive her. If she pours out her life for others as He did, she will have the opportunity of being treated as He was—from the Passion to the Resurrection. In the beautiful words of Saint John of the Cross, "Where there is no love, put love, and you will find love."[1]

CHALLENGES IN MARRIAGE

The statistics on marriage are quite discouraging. Many contracted marriages fail, leaving children to grow up without two committed parents in the home. The widespread availability of contraception and abortion undermines the ability of young people to grasp the concepts of fidelity, chastity and healthy communication. The sanctity of holy matrimony is widely misunderstood, as evidenced by the varied secular settings couples choose for their marriage ceremonies, by the confusion over same-sex unions and by the fact that many enter marriage without an openness to children and with an exit plan in place.

Girls are raised to be self-reliant and career-minded, often including husband and children only as afterthoughts or as part of a goal of self-actualization. The young woman is asked to be smart and clever, open and fun-loving, comfortable with men and yet well-suited to her single life. She may hope for marriage, but the men around her assume that she is sexually available with no strings attached. If she balks at "free love," she is labeled a prude or assumed to be maladjusted.

As ambivalent as a young woman may be toward a lifetime commitment, her male contemporaries are equally or more so. The leverage she may have had once—a man's desire for sexual intimacy—has long since evaporated with the ready availability of other women.

How can we blame a woman for some cynicism and forebodings about marital bliss? She must guard herself from all sorts of abuse. The children of broken homes have to be particularly wary, lacking helpful examples in their families. Often their peers have been poorly formed, and this doesn't help matters.

It is positively heroic for women to enter the wedded state with hearts prepared for unconditional love until death. Despite the fact that this is the only way that marriage can succeed—and the husband must share that attitude—popular culture conditions the young against such success.

CHALLENGES IN MOTHERHOOD

Who can know motherhood but a mother? How could anyone explain the quickening of a child in the womb, the ache of sorely taxed hips, the waves of labor pains, to one who hasn't given physical life to another? Even the most patient husband, listening with affection and gratitude, has little idea of the nature of this unique suffering.

On the other hand, what person can fathom the depths of joy that attend motherhood in its glories? Can anyone who is not a mother imagine the delights that come from the mere existence of one's offspring—not to mention the return of a smile, the earnest gifts or even the smallest of fulfilled expectations?

Being so richly entwined with another soul is beyond imagining, and yet inherent in it are countless opportunities for suffering. Physical harms run the gamut from the mundane to total oblation, should the mother lose her life through maternity-related complications. Not to be diminished is the range of emotional daggers that the folly of children brings, as the world, the flesh and the devil seek to devour them at every turn. Is it any wonder that women, now given the option through medical technologies, shrink from motherhood or limit the number of children to a very few?

The risks of loving are writ large for the woman choosing life, and who is there to remind her of the good? The mass media have other lifestyles to promote, since oblation and suffering don't sell well. There is no glut of happy, generous families to exemplify the possibilities. Society at large doesn't find virtue in vogue, nor does it foster commitment, stability or fidelity—all essential to the formation of children.

Fear is a backdrop for women as they wonder about the men in their lives, their future livelihood and the world their children would inherit. Fear is a monstrous obstacle to motherhood, rejecting it as a viable option or spoiling it as it unfolds, keeping a woman from giving her heart. We must address these very real fears as we promote life, motherhood and generosity, so that the way of Christ can be taken seriously.

Another factor affecting motherhood is the changing economic circumstances and societal expectations that have rearranged life so that women are an important part of the workforce. Many families have come to depend on two incomes, seriously affecting a woman's ability to embrace new life and even her choice to bond with her own infants.

It is essential that each woman consider her own circumstances and the needs of her loved ones, rather than casting an eye on her neighbor's state in life. She knows the grave concerns surrounding the decision to bear children: the financial concerns, the question of available time and resources, the demands that society has heaped on families everywhere.

A husband's fears can complicate the process, although he has been called to cooperate in the gift of new life. Some men have come to expect certain comforts; some are jealous for the little time and energy their wives have left after caring for children, home and other responsibilities; some lose sleep over the thought of additional dependents when their hard work brings limited pay; some fear additional burdens on the women they cherish. Stepping out in faith has practical dimensions that God recognizes, and "openness to life" presents concrete obstacles that bring their own suffering.

CHALLENGES IN THE CONSECRATED LIFE

Secular humanism has permeated Western culture for decades, and although the human heart yearns for the spiritual, much of it at present has been initiated and packaged in New Age vestments. This ideology ultimately twists spiritual longings back toward the self; worship of and commitment to a distinct Other are foreign. This, combined with materialism and the preeminence of the scientific, strongly discourages women from giving a gift of self though a consecrated vocation.

Feminism has made every effort to confuse the hierarchy of the Catholic Church with chauvinism. It has found the spousal nature of a sovereign "male" God suspect and bullied the ideal of handmaid and service out of young minds, claiming it is unfulfilling and demeaning. Couple this with the difficulty the young have with lifelong commitments of any sort, and it is easy to comprehend why the fields of consecrated life lie fallow.

Sadly, many women who gave generously of themselves to the consecrated life years ago found their communities wracked by confusion in the wake of the Second Vatican Council—confusion caused by misplaced zeal or a misunderstanding of the intentions of the Council fathers. Their prayer life, mission statements and habits changed drastically from what they had initially embraced, and their very vocation was subject to scrutiny. Now, decades later, they find their companions scattered, their new postulants few and insecurities tied to their advancing age growing. While some have embraced the changes that have washed over religious life, many have remained faithful to orders they hardly recognize.

BURNOUT

Finite creatures that we are, we can only give so much before we crash. The greatest affection for another soul can propel us but a limited distance before we run out of energy and desire. Love is demanding, even withering at times. Some situations—within the close quarters of family or community life, encompassing illness or dysfunctional personalities—can tax the most generous of souls.

If the woman is not intent on absorbing Christ and instead relies on her own love, her resources remain inadequate. If she has given up the attempt to see with His eyes, she will not see Him in the one she serves. If she slips away from prayer, she may not recognize the temptations of the evil one and be able to renounce him and his confusion. She finds herself drained and bitter at being used.

The woman must fortify herself with the sanctifying grace of God. While we all need to stay close to the sacraments, a person in a challenging environment must be constantly vigilant for ways to cling to God and discern His will in her life. Rendering her daily actions supernatural through union with God allows her to love through Him, with Him and in Him.

THE DOORMAT

Another danger in giving of self is that others soon recognize that generous nature. People are quick to discern that help is available, and the generous woman can find herself being used, taken for granted or walked upon because of her goodness of heart.

Once children know that mother can be relied upon for this favor or that good deal, it is hard for her to backtrack and refuse to give. Friends can take advantage of an easy source of childcare or items to borrow. Husbands too come to rely on women to meet their needs. Parents can be demanding and dependent on the children who help them, and coworkers are also sharp in dividing work, knowing who will and who won't complain. In light of this, it is understandable for a person to be slow to make offers for fear that she will sink into a state of abuse or inequality.

Two things must be considered in discerning when to give and when not to give. The first is the prayerful reflection on whether, in the long run, the gift actually benefits the recipient. For example, offering to help a child with a chore can be magnanimous when he or she is discouraged or overwhelmed, but to step in regularly and finish the work will only undermine essential lessons in responsibility, time management and accountability. Authentic love will separate acts of charity from enabling behaviors, which are far from loving and are damaging to other souls.

Secondly, when it is appropriate for a gift of self to be extended, the gift must be truly given—not taken. Many of our acts of charity are not offered in freedom but snatched from us out of obligation, guilt or a variety of other crippling mindsets. A mother who has not had time all year to contribute to her child's classroom may find herself grudgingly slathering icing on cupcakes well into the night in order to meet the expectations of others. A grown daughter and her family may feel obliged to go home for Sunday dinners week after week, to assure her mother she is loved—and to avoid a very unpleasant scene.

Despite these women's efforts, everyone suffers. Neither the cupcakes nor the visits are given in freedom; the grandmother senses her daughter's resentment and feels less loved than ever. Such efforts are like pieces of flesh torn out by others for the wrong reasons.

How many times do these dramas play out among well-meaning people? Granted, few gifts are given with complete purity of intention, but we would do well to remember Christ's statement to His disciples that no one *took* His life from Him, but that He laid it down of His own accord (see John 10:18). He laid it down for our salvation *as a gift*. It is said that His love alone would have bound Him to the cross if the soldiers had not provided the nails.

Falling into the trap of being a doormat is not inevitable. If the giver freely gives her time and treasure, if she is not motivated by the wrong intentions and if the gift enhances the life of the recipient, there will be no abuse by others, and the generosity of self will bless and fulfill the giver. Good friends can be invaluable sources of insight and perspective in helping us weigh different circumstances according to the standards of love and truth. Prayer is undoubtedly the richest wellspring of wisdom for discerning how and when to give to others.

FACING FRACTURED LIVES

Gaps in relationships are painful, and two tempting responses are to simply let them be or to increase the distance. Bringing together people at odds with one another is fraught with danger. To ask anyone to make it a part of her vocation to restore unity to injured parties is to ask a monumental thing, requiring prayer, sacrifice, dedication and energy.

Christ indeed bridged heaven and earth, and His bride the Church restores man to God and man to man on a regular basis. So must we women—despite the cost.

People from broken homes often settle for crumbs, since the original loaf has long been sundered. Many children in their early years become accustomed to splintered relationships and subtle wars, and they learn survival techniques to pull them through—techniques that are not always healthy in the long run. It is hard for these people to imagine fruits of harmony and authentic joy with those they know.

To ask women from broken homes to go out on a limb, risking even greater anger from those in their lives, would be madness were it not for the nature of love and the limitless possibilities of forgiveness. Many of these women own nothing but their resentments. Many reject God based on the events of their lives. Many are terrified of stepping out in faith toward the Unknown. Many have never tasted true freedom and cannot imagine that it is a gift for the asking.

It is imperative—for their own good and the good of the

wider community—that these women embrace the deep and total healing that is possible in Christ Jesus. Only then can they receive the human person in the way he or she should be received. If we cannot receive the person—we to whom the human person first is entrusted—then how can we bring men to do so? If our view of love and commitment is laced with cynicism, how can the world grow closer to God?

When a woman senses barriers between herself and others, or if she realizes that she cannot look another in the eye and see a person worthy of love and respect, she must make every effort to discover why. Recognizing the valid concerns outlined above, it is only reasonable that she might fear the demands that such love would make on her. It's possible that she doesn't recognize the meaning or nature of authentic love; deep down she might find those who choose differently to be an inherent threat to her and her own choices; or she may bear the unhealed wounds of past misguided relationships.

In all of this Christ loves her passionately and wants her at peace. Gentle, patient and with tender mercy, He asks that she take the time and effort to go to the root of the problem, to name her sorrows and to lay them at His feet. To help in this path of self-discovery, Pope John Paul II highlighted how the lives of women in general have often been made difficult by systemic abuses:

> Unfortunately, we are heirs to a history which has *conditioned* us to a remarkable extent. In every time and place, this conditioning has been an obstacle to the progress of women. Women's dignity has often been unacknowledged and their prerogatives misrepresented; they have often been relegated to the margins of society and even reduced to servitude.... And if objective blame, especially in particular

historical contexts, has belonged to not just a few members of the Church, for this I am truly sorry. May this regret be transformed, on the part of the whole Church, into a renewed commitment of fidelity to the Gospel vision. When it comes to setting women free from every kind of exploitation and domination, the Gospel contains an ever relevant message which goes back to the *attitude of Jesus Christ himself.*[2]

A life of faith, based on a close sacramental relationship with Christ Jesus, offers every woman a richer life and joy beyond her imagination. She can link her inevitable sufferings intimately to His redemptive cross. She can lay her burdens at the foot of that cross. There she is free to end her patterns of dysfunction and to begin to pursue her vocation of loving and receiving love according to God's plan.

FORGIVENESS: THE ONLY ANSWER

Fear is the greatest obstacle to love. To love without measure means to step out into the great unknown and to take the risk of being hurt, rejected or humiliated or of losing the beloved outright. Christ took all of these risks with His creatures and demands that we do so as well. The wounds and scars from love gone awry do not release us from the demands of discipleship but remind us of the constant need to forgive.

For such a simple and straightforward concept, forgiveness can be quite misunderstood. At its very heart it implies a response to injustice or injury, whether or not the one harming the other realizes what he has done. Some childhood slights may now seem unreasonable or trifling, but they hurt nevertheless at the time. Some pain is inflicted through malice, some through neglect or ignorance. Some pain is fleeting; some is carried to the grave. Personalities within families are often difficult, marriage sometimes occasions nearly insurmountable conflicts and associations within the world at large reveal harsh realities in which many suffer. All in all, daily life bears within it abundant opportunities to forgive in order to allow harmony to prevail.

Forgiveness is not a means of glossing over pain or pretending that all is well. It acknowledges injury and moves toward the only Christian response: "You have hurt me; in the name of Christ I forgive you."

There is no unforgivable act, no unpardonable offense. If God Himself can forgive man's rejection of the Son, there is nothing we can hold bound without risking hell itself. Hell is a very real consequence of the lack of forgiveness, but the glorious gift of forgiveness is peace in this life. It only takes an act of the will, regardless of the emotions involved or the lack of affection for the one who has caused the harm.

In fact, the victim need never confront the one who hurt her. Grace can pour in with a firm intention and the words to accompany it: "I forgive this person for the way he hurt me." God will do the rest.

When a person experiences the deep peace that flows from letting go of resentments and embracing forgiveness, she is far more inclined to reach out to others in love. With increasing confidence she can undertake the risks associated with giving for the good of others and doing the hard work that accompanies such a gift of self. Knowing that God has forgiven her, that He led by example in forgiving from the cross those who would not receive His love and that His grace is always available for the constant steps of forgiveness still to be taken, the enormous pitfalls that discourage her from reaching out to others diminish until they become inconsequential to her everyday actions.

Her childhood wounds, her many disappointments and the rejections that she has faced no longer cripple her, no longer prohibit her from answering God's call to love. Buried in the wounds of Christ and His companionship through the Eucharist, she will find that joy replaces fear and supernatural purpose colors each encounter with others.

Saint Josephine Bakhita can teach us many things about the authentic freedom that flows from forgiveness. Born in Sudan, at age nine she was kidnapped from a warm and loving family by slave traders. She was sold five times over the next few years.

Her fourth owner chose to "decorate" her, as was the custom of the day. With a sharp razor blade, designs were cut into Bakhita's skin in artistic patterns—along her limbs, across her torso, 114 images in all—and then salt was poured into the wounds to cause the skin around the incisions to curl back. Flour finished the job of discoloration, so that the patterns would remain white against her dark skin.

Bakhita lay for weeks in delirium as she underwent this lengthy torture, at death's door all the while. In addition to this degradation, for years afterward she was regularly beaten and was afforded neither basic human respect nor dignified treatment.

It was her fifth owner, the Italian consul at Khartoum, who first showed her kindness. He ultimately brought her to Europe, where she discovered Christ. While taking care of the young daughter of a family there, she was introduced to the Canossian Sisters, with whom she eventually found a home as a religious sister. Fifty years of quiet consecrated life allowed her to manifest the deep abiding peace that faith and forgiveness can bring.

Seeing God's hand even in the difficult path of her life, she noted, "If I was to meet those slave raiders that abducted me and those who tortured me, I'd kneel down to them to kiss their hands, because, if it had not been for them, I would not have become a Christian and religious woman."[3] Note that she didn't say that what the slave traders and her owners did to her was right; it most certainly was not. But she recognized that through her wounds she found salvation, and this she could not ignore.

At Bakhita's beatification Pope John Paul II praised her as

"Our Universal Sister," pointing out that she offers us "a message of reconciliation and evangelic forgiveness in a world so much divided and hurt by hatred and violence."[4]

There are many forms of slavery; some do not have visible chains or leave outward marks. We suffer from them as long as we cannot name them, claim our own dignity of being created in the image and likeness of God and renounce them from holding us captive.

The liberation that forgiveness can offer is as stark as the sundering of iron fetters and the opening of a prison door. It is for the one who suffers to choose freedom and wholeness of heart, despite her surroundings. The graces of God are available to all even in the darkest hours, and each cross bears within it the seeds of Easter for those who cling to Christ.

Most of the saints of God have stories of suffering and rejection. Studying their lives will strengthen our resolve to follow the path of forgiveness as a means of peacefully navigating life in this world. While all people undergo suffering in life, there are only two responses: pain and fear, or forgiveness and freedom. Radical love requires radical action. Certainly, dwelling on pain and resentments doesn't work; on the other hand, Christ's way of forgiveness will change the landscape—both in this life and the next.

CHAPTER TEN

Our Gift to the Church and to the World

It is essential to ponder the ways God is always present and the means He offers of pulling away from the path of sin that seems so entrenched in a given generation. When a people slides gradually deeper into an excess or vice, the only workable way to breathe grace back into the culture is to cleave to its opposite virtue. If we consider the challenges of two particularly well-known times in Christian history, this method will become clear.

OPPORTUNITIES IN CHAOS

As the Roman Empire disintegrated and suffered the implosion of its societal structures, foreign tribes arrived from all directions, bringing in those who were unfamiliar with the culture of that civilization and either indifferent or hostile to its treasures. They invaded a prostrate and weakened land and had little to offer from their own way of life to rebuild a comparable culture. In the ensuing chaos the Catholic Church was given a tremendous opportunity.

It had only been under the Emperor Constantine in the early fourth century that the Church had moved from being a persecuted body of believers living in the shadows of society to being the official religion of the Empire. Within a few hundred years the Church could offer the stability of monastic life, which had grown quietly both before and after Benedict wrote his Rule in the sixth century. As monasteries and convents grew in number, they filled the void left by the crumbling Roman institutions and carried forth the body of knowledge that the new rulers scorned. The monastics were responsible for a gradual infusion of gospel values into their surroundings, an understanding of family life that respected all of its members, an ordering of the day around prayer and liturgy, an educational model that shared the wisdom of both the Church and antiquity and a strong agricultural foundation to support the population year-round. It was just what the people needed at that time, and these orders blossomed in the wake of chaos and deprivation.

Another example comes from the twelfth and thirteenth centuries. At this time the Christian culture built over the previous half millennium had lost its moral center. Europe was materially wealthy and steeped in an external Catholic culture but was no longer focused on the Person of Christ. The entrenched structures began once again to decay, as the Church hierarchy used its influence for power and corrupt gain, and a culture overly familiar with the gospel took its message for granted.

Into this void stepped Francis of Assisi—his total poverty the only adequate remedy to the excesses of his age. While many reenergized missionaries preached the message of Christ, it was as much the personal witness of the growing band of Franciscans as it was the words from any pulpit that brought the culture back to authentic Christianity. Francis and his brothers, with Clare and her sisters, epitomized a vibrant image of Christ that spoke in a fresh way to their bored contemporaries. To them love was more than simply a word or a concept: It was a total embrace, showing absolute trust in divine Providence. These men and women committed themselves to a radical separation from the comforts of the world in order to show that such things were superfluous to those given wholly to God.

OUR CURRENT CHALLENGE

The previous examples show us that extraordinary application of the appropriate virtue will bring about a healthy culture even in the most extreme circumstances. With confidence we must look at our own generation and discern the predominant fault at its heart. Few would dispute the conclusion that one enormous challenge is the rampant promiscuity in our midst. This is combined with a disdain for stable family life permeating academia, the mass media and the entertainment industry.

Children are at the heart of the battle. Popular culture steadfastly refuses to acknowledge that a healthy marriage provides the best environment for them. Pre-adolescents are regularly entertained with vulgar and vacuous films that lampoon traditional values and mock those who live by them. Even the concept of "education in virtue" is derided. Few in positions of influence are truly fighting for what is in the best interest of young people, seeing them first and foremost as potential consumers.

While women and children are the primary victims of the sexual heresies of our day, they are the very key to conquering them. In light of the examples above, where order was the opposite of chaos and poverty the opposite of material excess, *the antidote to sexual perversion is purity*.

Because of the nature of sexual appetites and conquest, women who understand purity and commitment are the key component to building the culture of life. The ideal culture will naturally respect the family as the most reliable guardian of the human person and lifelong marriage as the only environment for the sexual embrace. Women are capable of rolling back the wanton disregard for their integral beauty by promoting modesty at every opportunity and offering the world authentic femininity. Women who truly guard the children entrusted to them will take care that these children are not assaulted with inappropriate images or tempted to use sex as leverage or entertainment. Women can use their gift of being able to connect with others on a deep and human level to offer authentic wisdom about the human person and his or her place in God's plan.

This charge to women in no way exonerates men of using people as objects. There is enough blame to go around to most members of our society. It just so happens that, at this time in history, a key element to fighting the immorality we are facing is the *purity of women*.

Far from passively embracing their victimization as inevitable, women must take the lead in transforming the culture. For whatever good they provide, government programs and even preaching will not suffice. To recall for our purposes the essential quote of the council fathers, at this time "women imbued with the Gospel will do so much to aid mankind in not falling."[1] Just as the stability of the monks provided their witness to a continent in disarray, and *il poverello* was the antidote to the pride and power of a bloated hierarchy, chaste and joyful women in this age are called to initiate the restoration of wholesome family life and respect for the human person by faithfully imaging the bride.

CHRIST'S HOPE FOR HIS CHURCH

While it would be wonderful to restore stability to family life and establish a profound respect for God's gift of sexuality, there is an additional benefit to having women understand and live authentic femininity. To enter more deeply into the paradigm of "woman imaging the Church," we must consider the greatest scandal to the world today: the lack of unity within the mystical body of Christ.

Jesus' final discourse before His Passion was on the one topic that defined both the inner working of the Trinity and the nature of the embrace between Christ and His bride: unity.

"That they may be one" (John 17:21–22) was Christ's ardent desire. The fact that His followers have splintered into factions is an abomination to the rest of the world, and it saps the bride of her strength and vigor.

As any mother of a broken family can attest, a heart reaching across divides suffers enormously and dissipates energy necessary to loving into a variety of complicated strategies. Conversations run the risk of becoming battles, activities bear an underlying strain, and tension spoils encounters that should be filled with joy. The lack of unity carries its accompanying baggage on every level—in the family, in the workplace, in neighborhoods, even to armed struggle in various settings.

One extraordinary dimension of the theology of the body as it is being revealed in this present age is its potential to heal this very disunity within the mystical body of Christ. It is undeniable that there are widespread differences between the various Christian sects on the understanding of Christ, the nature of the Trinity and the interplay between faith and works, to name but a few issues. Yet while millions of the faithful argue about various points of theology and possible meanings of authority, those who passionately love God as He is revealed in Holy Scripture can at least agree on the nature of the family and the need to live in virtue.

"Politics makes strange bedfellows," they say. You may have noticed that we have been gradually surrounded and marginalized by secular forces who reject *all* religious concepts in the marketplace of ideas. As the faithful pause to take a breath in their internecine debates, they realize that the greater threat to the faith is the widespread notion that there is no God, that family is what man defines for himself, that sexuality is a drive that is to be harnessed and enjoyed apart from its God-given ends and that the human person has no particular dignity in the order of creation.

Even those who defend the occasional necessity of divorce

and remarriage must take stock of the fact that serial marriages and couples living together without benefit of marriage are part of the current trend. We also see same-sex attraction redefined as a legitimate and healthy "lifestyle." While many Christians publicly or privately have made peace with contraception as a valid moral option and abortion as a private "choice," they too have to come to grips with skyrocketing rates of teen sex and broken marriages, not to mention the millions of babies killed yearly.

These sobering realities—especially the alarming statistics concerning family life, sexually transmitted diseases and suicide rates—combined with widespread moral relativism are having the positive effect of uniting those of goodwill. It is said, "There are no denominations in gulags," and we find ourselves in a similar position. It was on the picket lines and subsequently in the prison cells during the Operation Rescue movement that Christians of many denominations prayed together and shared testimonies of faith. It is in banding together in grassroots efforts to fight secularism and pornography that conversations about common ground in the faith begin.

In short, the evil proposed by those who refuse to live according to God's will is trumping the evil of disunity among believers. Opposition to this evil can fuse believers into a strong band of faithful. In the battle to restore dignity to womanhood and respect to life, women can contribute a great deal toward the restoration of the unity that Christ wants. And the sooner they grasp that truth, the sooner mankind will know peace.

LITURGICAL TRUTHS REVEALED IN THE FAMILY

If through prayer and study we can discern the nuptial meaning of the body and the mystical relationship between Christ and His bride, the Church, we will begin to recognize the interplay between the sacred and the mundane. God is revealing to the

Church at this critical time the connections between the way we live masculinity, femininity, family life and sexuality on one hand and the liturgy, the sacramental system and the world of grace on the other. Stereotypes are being ripped away as the essence of such things is becoming manifest.

As these revelations come to light in the coming years, imagine the gift to the world if, beyond the rhetoric, all people could see shining examples of the bride reflecting the will of her Spouse. Those who would not darken a church door would encounter God in the street, the classroom and the home. Those who have not been introduced to Christ would find Him echoed in conversation, even in a passing greeting. Those whose preconceived notions of the corruption of hierarchies keep them away from all things religious would be disarmed by authentic motherly affection with only their best interests at heart.

This is not to pit "male" and "female" images against one another, as though the former were unworkable and the latter pure. Just as man and woman are called into a relationship based on complementarity, the male hierarchy and the bridal Church are both essential for a full understanding of the deposit of faith. The argument, rather, is that the human person is entrusted in a particular way to the woman to be nurtured, that she is the gatekeeper to certain inherent truths and that when she affirms those in her path with genuine selfless affection, they are drawn toward those truths in a childlike way.

In an age when womanhood has suffered grievously from defilement—from both outward abuses and self-inflicted lies—only purification of that corruption can lead souls back to the truth. What will arise from this purification will be a greater, deeper and more profound femininity than ever before. The effects that these women, focused on Christ, can have on their surroundings will be enormous. When enough women base their lives on their true calling, rifts will heal on every level.

It would be naïve to imagine that all heresy and all disobedience would vanish from this world. To think that possible would be to misread human nature and the effects of sin on our lives. Yet we can make the case that there is a proportional relationship between fidelity of women to their vocations—through the new insights into the theology of the body, which God offers to us at this critical juncture—and the union of those who follow Christ with His visible representative on earth. This is directly linked to the vision of His bride that Christ so eloquently offered before He laid down His life for her. The answer to the challenges to Church teaching on marriage, procreation and personhood will result in a more profound explanation of male and female.

THE ORDER OF LOVE

There is a key point in *Mulieris Dignitatem* that cannot be overlooked. All of creation is subject to order; even the Trinity bears within Itself a procession, a means by which one Person relates to Another. Beyond that, on every level there is an inherent nature to all created things that we must respect in order to live in the truth.

The most important currency in the universe, the only means of exchange that will last unto all eternity, is love. Of the three virtues that touch God—faith, hope and love—love is the one that will never stop existing, for it is the essence of God Himself as well as the means to find Him.

Interestingly enough, in the order of the universe, in the procession of love, woman comes before man. As Pope John Paul II wrote:

> In God's eternal plan, woman is the one in whom the order of love in the created world of persons takes first root.... When the author of the Letter to the Ephesians calls Christ "the Bridegroom" and the Church "the Bride," he indirectly confirms through this analogy *the*

truth about woman as bride. The Bridegroom is the one who loves. The Bride is loved: *it is she who receives love, in order to love in return.*[2]

Thus God would have woman subject to legitimate male authority, as a bride submits to her bridegroom. Yet in the heavenly procession, love proceeds from the Father, through the Holy Spirit, *to woman,* who in turn distributes it to all of mankind. This is based on the receptivity inherent to her femininity and her primordial intimacy with the human person, which is at the heart of her vocation, no matter how she lives her life.

This is an awesome privilege and a tremendous responsibility. It is actually even beyond the imaginations of most of the women who agitate for worldly power or secular kinds of authority. It places in the hands of women, first and foremost, love— the most cherished element of the universe—for her to use for the building of the kingdom of God.

On the reverse side this means that any woman who is incapable of transmitting love to those in her domain is primarily responsible for their diminishment. We bear a double-edged sword in the way that we interact with others—either bringing them closer to God or creating an obstacle. The ideal is for us to be transparent enough to allow the light of Christ, the ultimate Bridegroom, to shine forth to transform souls and to reveal His creative love.

If John the Baptist recognized that "He must increase, but I must decrease" (John 3:30), how much more should the woman, who receives new life and forms children by her side? How much more the woman, who eases the burden of the sick and suffering? How much more the woman, who creates a respite for weary souls on pilgrimage to their Father?

The Church, as bride, has always been understood to be feminine—in fact, all creation is feminine in relationship to God because of its receptiveness to His creative and loving initiative.

Vatican II confirmed this hallowed interpretation, as John Paul II noted in *Mulieris Dignitatem*: "[I]n the hierarchy of holiness it is *precisely the 'woman,'* Mary of Nazareth, who is the 'figure' of the Church. She 'precedes' everyone on the path to holiness."[3] Thus, just as the bridal image takes precedence over the "Petrine" image, which gives the Church its essential hierarchy (see CCC, 773), the response to God should first be understood and lived by women. If they, being the epitome of God's incarnate bride, can understand their vocation to love, then order in the created world can be that much more perfectly restored.

If Catholic women can transmit the joy of responding in love to women of all faiths, the rest of the divisions will disintegrate by comparison. This is all part of God's wise plan. He provides the grace, the strength and the holy audacity to step out in faith to restore unity among believers and to draw the world to that radiant bride.

ONE, HOLY, CATHOLIC AND APOSTOLIC CHURCH

Throughout this book I have shown that each of the four marks of the Church will be strengthened through the restoration of authentic femininity.

1. The one bride and her undivided love for her Beloved will make possible unity in the Christian churches.

2. The holy woman will restore dignity to the human person through her personal contact, her visible influence and her prayers.

3. The catholicity of the Church will radiate from every woman who joins her unique path to the singular mission of the true bride.

4. The Church's apostolic link through the ages will now be confidently lived out in the lives of myriad women, who will attach themselves to the authentic bride, mirroring her fruitful spousal love.

These are bold promises, but they simply reflect God's own word and the mandate He gave us to build His kingdom on earth. Trust and surrender to the plan of God will provide the peace and joy that we've been searching for in many places. And marvelously enough, we don't even need to go outside of ourselves to find the mission—we *are* the mission as God would have it in this age. We only need to take our femininity in its purest form and cleave with it to the cross for the good of all.

Christ reiterated His command "Fear not" (Matthew 10:31) more often than any other command in Scripture. Women are in a sufficiently vulnerable position, overall in life, to experience fear. They are subject to the pains and potential dangers of childbirth, the concern for children and possible physical and emotional abuse from many quarters.

As I previously mentioned, fear is usually at the core of a woman's "no" to God's plan for her life. This rejection of God's will is often tied to a secular cry for help and protection, and the stopgap measures to gain them only exacerbate woman's vulnerability in the long term.

If women can overcome fear and can trust in God and His promises, everyone can.

LOOK TO MARY

Our model for courage must be the young woman God ordained from the beginning to crush the head of the serpent, who never deviated from His will nor withheld her love in any circumstance.

Understanding the Blessed Virgin Mary is integral to understanding authentic femininity. As daughter of God the Father, mother of God the Son and spouse of the Holy Spirit, her position within the mystery of the Trinity might seem to place her beyond our understanding and emulation—but that is not so. God in His goodness offers us a woman who walked and wept, who laughed and lingered among loved ones as all of us do. While she was without sin, she was flesh and blood, wife and friend, mother and believer—in a capacity we can all treasure on a variety of levels.

The fact that Mary progressed from daughter to wife and from mother to widow gives us much to appreciate about her pilgrimage of faith. She offers an example of holiness in so many vocations that all women can find common ground with at least a portion of her life on earth. Like all of us, she stepped out in faith, unsure of where her path would lead but fully confident in the plan of God yet to be revealed.

Mary's quiet life was occasionally punctuated by events beyond the ordinary, but she was grounded enough in the inner life of God to maintain a peaceful calm. This grounding came from the fact that she centered her life around the rhythms of the Jewish religious observances of her day. As a part of the chosen people, she was familiar with the Scriptures, and she took God at His word. Thankfully for all people, when the time came for His word to take flesh, she said yes.

So while Mary's powerful intercession with God is available to all who call upon her, her life itself is a valuable lesson that we can study for insights. Her waiting, her acting, her speaking, her silences, all offer us images of holiness. As the perfect woman, honored with the title "Seat of Wisdom," she teaches us how to live femininity in all its fullness. Her docility to the will of God brought forth the means of our salvation. She is theologically rich, philosophically pure but also—thankfully for us—

practically accessible. God is generous, and in Mary we find enough to ponder for a lifetime.

In imitation of both the Blessed Virgin Mary and the Church, each woman finds her mission in building up the kingdom of the Father so that when the Bridegroom arrives, all will be ready for Him. Her heart of love, her desire to serve, her embrace of the gospel message and her joyful ability to receive the abundant graces of her Creator ensure that life—natural and supernatural—will find rich soil.

When Christ comes, will He find any faith on earth (see Luke 18:8)? The answer will be in direct correlation to the willingness of each woman to embrace her vocation and bring the Bridegroom the harvest that is by rights His very own. And remarkably, inherent in God's justice is the rich truth that we cannot achieve our salvation and joy any other way.

Epilogue

This book is an invitation to my brothers and sisters in Christ to delve more deeply into the ways that women can image the bride of Christ, Holy Mother Church, with their very lives. While I hope that the framework is comprehensive enough to direct the inquiry, it only scratches the surface of this marvelous topic. It is incumbent on us to probe the subject more deeply in the coming years, to study the implications of the theology of the body and thus to unlock the treasures God has imbedded in His own creation.

The Scriptures are full of images of the chasm between the light and the darkness. Light, of course, is a reference to Christ Himself (see John 8:12). The virgins in the parable were to greet their lord with lighted lamps (see Matthew 25:5–10), and so do we embrace our vocation as handmaidens. Just as the wisdom that the Church transmits is founded in God, the brightness we bear into the world in our lamps is set off by the divine sparks of spousal love.

It is a small start, but that is how Christendom began. What is fading must be reinvigorated, and women are key to shaping the restoration of God's truth to the world through authentic femininity.

Jesus warned, "When you see Jerusalem surrounded by armies, then know that its desolation has come near" (Luke 21:20). But we know that desolation is *not* the end of the story. "After that tribulation,…the powers in the heavens will be shaken. And then they will see the Son of man coming in clouds with great power and glory" (Mark 13: 24–26).

Every woman can do her part to restore the image of the bride. Women together can embrace motherhood in all its forms: nourishing, teaching, building bridges, healing, confirming the beauty in souls, forgiving, building Christian culture in myriad ways and radiating purity. Thus they give flesh to Holy Mother Church for the world to see.

Each concrete action grounded in prayer is a spiritual torch. What could be lovelier than these women in procession—responding to the call *Marana 'tha*!—"Behold, the bridegroom! Come out to meet him" (Matthew 25:6). With haste we must prepare to greet the Beloved, before whose throne we will lay our torches, creating a bonfire of authentic, purifying, life-giving love. This is the unique call to women, and this is our tremendous opportunity, for God wants to embrace us with His perfect, *nuptial* love, which has poured out from all eternity and will continue even unto the consummation of the world.

As He said, "I have come to bring fire to the earth, and how I wish it were blazing already!" (Luke 12:49, *The Jerusalem Bible*). *Deo gratias*!

Notes

Foreword

1. John Paul II, Apostolic Letter *Mulieris Dignitatem*, "On the Dignity and Vocation of Women on the Occasion of the Marian Year," August 15, 1988, no. 4, as quoted in John Paul II, *Theology of the Body* (Boston: Pauline, 1997), p. 447.

2. John Paul II, Encyclical Letter *Evangelium Vitae*, "The Gospel of Life," no. 99, as quoted in *Theology of the Body*, p. 570.

Chapter One: The Essence of Femininity

1. Second Vatican Council, "Closing Message to Women," in Walter M. Abbott, ed., *The Documents of Vatican II* (New York: Guild, 1967), p. 733.

2. William Wordsworth, "Hymn to the Virgin" (1822).

3. John Paul II, Address at the Church of St. Sopra Minerva, Rome, November 5, 1978, as quoted in *L'Osservatore Romano*, November 16, 1978.

Chapter Two: Mirroring the Sacraments of Initiation

1. The old (and seemingly trite) platitude of "Offer it up!" is laden with rich theology, reminding us that we can participate in Christ's work of salvation.

2. Gianna Emanuela Molla, address to the Second International Celebration of the Family, Maracana Stadium in Brazil, October 1997, as quoted in *Canticle*, vol. 6 (Autumn 1999), p. 35.

3. John Paul II, comments at the beatification ceremony for Blessed Gianna, April 24, 1994, in *Canticle*, vol. 6, p. 35. Gianna was canonized on May 16, 2005.

4. Incidentally, this was Rosalind's final obstacle to Catholic faith. The answer was so compelling that she not only has joined the Church but has spent years evangelizing around the world.

5. Etiquette is covered at greater length in chapter eight.

6. *American Heritage Dictionary* (New York: Dell, 1994), p. 183.

7. John Paul II, *Mulieris Dignitatem*, no. 18, as quoted in *Theology of the Body*, p. 470.

8. In preparation for the Jubilee year of 2000, Pope John Paul II systematically asked forgiveness on behalf of the Church for these errors over the centuries, which is the only answer for such injustices against personal or cultural integrity.

Chapter Three: Mirroring the Sacraments of Healing

1. Irina Ilovaisky Giorgi-Alberti, Address to the Twelfth General Congregation of the Synod of Bishops, October 8, 1999, www.zenit.org.

2. "High" Anglicans and those practicing in the Anglo-Catholic traditions have retained religious life for men and women and even in some instances the sacraments of confession and extreme unction, although all are quite rare. The point being made is that even if limited opportunities were available to women, they were not a part of the religious landscape for widespread appreciation. For more on religious orders of women who nursed near battlefields, see Ruth Lasseter, "Saints at War," *Canticle*, vol. 7, pp. 10–13. http://www.hawthorne-dominicans.org.

Chapter Four: Spousal Love

1. Joseph Ratzinger, "The Ministry and Life of Priests," lecture given October 1995, trans. Edward G. Maristany and Gerald Malsbary, reprinted in *Homiletic and Pastoral Review*, August-September 1997.

2. Ratzinger.

3. The same theology that bars women from holy orders defines marriage as a lifelong union between one man and one woman. To reject this foundation shared by the two sacraments is to support "same-sex unions," which are both anathema to the revealed truths of God and sterile.

4. Compare to DS 1800; CIC, can. 1055 §2.

5. John Paul II, Apostolic Exhortation *Vita Consecrata*, "On the Consecrated Life and Its Mission in the Church and in the World," March 25, 1996, no. 1.

6. Elizabeth Kuhns, *The Habit: A History of the Catholic Nuns* (New York: Doubleday, 2003), p. 2.

7. Edith Stein, *Essays on Women*, trans. Freda Mary Oben (Washington: ICS, 1996), p. 31.

8. John Paul II, *Vita Consecrata*, no. 7.

9. John Paul II, *Vita Consecrata*, no. 3.

10 John Paul II, *Vita Consecrata*, no. 29.

11. John Paul II, *Vita Consecrata*, no. 6.

12. John Paul II, *Vita Consecrata*, no. 105.

13. John Paul II, *Vita Consecrata*, no. 15.

14. John Paul II, *Vita Consecrata*, no. 18.

15. John Paul II, *Vita Consecrata*, no. 28.

16. John Paul II, *Vita Consecrata*, no. 34.

Chapter Five: The Church as Mother

1. Louis Bouyer, *Woman in the Church* (San Francisco: Ignatius, 1984), p. 52.

2. John Paul II, Encyclical Letter *Redemptoris Mater*, "On the Blessed Virgin Mary in the Life of the Pilgrim Church," March 25, 1987, no. 23.

3. Second Vatican Council, *Lumen Gentium*, no. 62, in Abbott, p. 91.

Chapter Six: The Church as Teacher

1. Elizabeth Heubeck, "How Male and Female Brains Differ," www.webmd.com.

2. John Paul II, "Letter to Women," June 29, 1995, nos. 10, 11.

3. See Francis Martin, *The Feminist Question: Feminist Theology in the Light of Christian Tradition* (Grand Rapids, Mich.: Eerdmans, 1994), p. 49.

4. Martin, p. 49.

153

5. Martin, p. 49.

6. Fundamental principle attributed to Aristotle. See Saint Thomas Aquinas, *Summa Theologica*, I, Q. lxxviii, a. 3; Q. lxxix, a. 2.

7. "Maria Montessori," www.webster.edu.

8. Maria Montessori, *The Absorbent Mind*, trans. Claude A. Claremont (New York: Holt, Rinehart and Winston, 1967), p. 150.

9. E. Mortimer Standing, "Maria Montessori: An Appreciation," *Westminster Cathedral Chronicle*, June 1952, p. 1, as quoted in Pat Davis, "What Is Montessori?" www.montessori-academy.org.

10. Robert G. Buckenmeyer, "Principles of Pre-Primary Education According to Maria Montessori," www.transporter.com.

11. Freda Mary Oben, *The Life and Thought of St. Edith Stein* (New York: Alba, 2001), p. 81.

12. Stein, p. 45.

Chapter Seven: The Bride in the Old Testament

1. See Christoph Schönborn, *Loving the Church* (San Francisco: Ignatius, 1998), p. 146.

2. Roland E. Murphy, O.CARM., *The Tree of Life: An Exploration of Biblical Wisdom Literature*, third ed. (Grand Rapids, Mich.: 1996). pp. 133-134.

3. Schönborn, p. 96.

4. Feminism has adulterated some Jewish communities, allowing women to pay similar homage to the Torah and thus style themselves as "brides of the Torah." The meaning becomes lost when women "marry" their own image. If women understood the honor incumbent in "being wisdom," they would not "step down" to offer chivalric service to wisdom.

5. It was Uzzah who reached out to steady the ark when the oxen stumbled. "And the anger of the LORD was kindled against Uzzah; and God smote him there because he put forth his hand to the ark; and he died there beside the ark of God" (2 Samuel 6:7).

6. Recall the importance of gates for sanctuaries in chapter four.

7. Irene Nowell, *Women in the Old Testament* (Collegeville, Minn.: Liturgical, 1997), p. 140; see Proverbs 1—9.

Chapter Eight: The Church as Builder of Culture

1. Joseph Pieper, *Leisure: The Basis of Culture* (New York: Random, 1963), pp. 56–59.

2. George Weigel, *Witness to Hope: The Biography of Pope John Paul II* (New York: HarperCollins, 1999), p. 262.

3. John Paul II, *Evangelium Vitae*, no. 99, as quoted in *Theology of the Body*, p. 570.

4. John Paul II, *Evangelium Vitae*, no. 99, as quoted in *Theology of the Body*, p. 571.

5. Robert Louis Wilken, "The Church as Culture," *First Things*, April 2004, p. 32.

6. Wilken, pp. 31–36.

7. Stein, *Essays on Woman*, p. 57.

8. Open, pp. 83–84.

9. Dom Jean-Baptiste Chautard, *The Soul of the Apostolate* (Rockford, Ill.: TAN, 1974), p. 53.

10. Henri de Lubac, *The Splendor of the Church* (San Francisco: Ignatius, 1999), p. 43.

11. de Lubac, p. 42.

12. Preface for Advent 1.

13. Wilken, p. 36.

Chapter Nine: Pitfalls to Authentic Femininity

1. Saint John of the Cross, http://saints.catholic.org.

2. John Paul II, *Letter to Women*, no. 3.

3. Afrol News, "Josephine Bakhita: An African Saint," www.afrol.com.

4. John Paul II, address at Blessed Bakhita's beatification, May 17, 1992, as quoted in "Josephine Bakhita: An African Saint."

Chapter Ten: Our Gift to the Church and to the World

1. "Closing Message to Women," in Abbott, p. 733.

2. John Paul II, *Mulieris Dignitatem*, no. 29, as quoted in *Theology of the Body*, p. 484.

3. John Paul II, *Mulieris Dignitatem*, no. 27, as quoted in *Theology of the Body*, p. 482.